I0442109

The
Gay Agenda
2013

All In

Juan Ahonen-Jover, Ph.D.

Published by **create**space

Book website: www.GayAgenda2013.com

Dedication

This book is for all persons who
believe in the equality expressed in the
United States Declaration of Independence—

**"We hold these truths to be self-evident, that all men are
created equal"**—

and in the United States Constitution:

**"Nor deny to any person within its jurisdiction the equal
protection of the laws."**

Books in This Series

The Gay Agenda 2012: All Out

The Gay Agenda 2013: All In

The Gay Agenda is a comprehensive guidebook for achieving legal equality for lesbian, gay, bisexual, and transgender Americans. The only book like it, it gets updated yearly with specific action plans for that year.

What Readers Are Saying

"WOW - what a huge addition (both in terms of amount of work you did and in terms of usefulness). It's a great roadmap for people to use."

"As your previous book, well done and important to help stimulate action, empower the activists, and help focus on reality without destroying visions of the future."

"You have certainly tackled a HUGE and BROAD topic and done a marvelous job."

"It is a compendium/combination of all of the following: an Op Ed, a manual, encyclopedia article, memoir, pep talk."

"The book will be a wonderful resource to anyone who cares about achieving full equality."

"It may be the first book that tells the unvarnished truth!"

"It is definitely an easy read since the chapters are only two or three pages long!"

"I'm impressed."

"Such a terrific project, book, contribution!!!!"

Is This Book for *You?*

This book is for believers only. Do you firmly believe in the principle of treating everybody equally under the law?

- If you are seeking to understand the most important social issue of our generation, this book is for you (especially Part I and the epilogue).

- If you are a parent or grandparent interested in family values and protecting your children, this book is for you (especially Parts I, II, and the epilogue).

- If you are a policy maker, independently of party affiliation, who wants to write laws that are fair, this book is for you (read it all).

- If you are a religious person interested in preserving your freedom of religion, this book is for you (especially Part I and the epilogue).

- If your sexual orientation or gender identity or expression does not fit that of the majority, this book is for you. You may know some of the information presented, but you will gain insights and inspiration for fighting for equal treatment under the law (so read it all and *take action*).

- If you are a believer in equality, this book is for you. You may know some of the book's content, but read it all and *take action.*

- If you have read the 2012 edition of *The Gay Agenda*, read Part IV in detail since it is completely new and describes the actions to take in 2013.

Contents

Preface

In the United States, our core beliefs are under attack. Freedom of religion is under attack. Family values are under attack. Individualism and the pursuit of happiness are under attack. The courts are under attack.

The Gay Agenda book series is for people who believe in the core principle of our Constitution: to be treated equally under the law. What would it be like if we could return to the vision of our great Constitution? A vision of freedom, including freedom of religion and freedom to individuality.

The *Gay Agenda 2013: All In* describes the gay agenda for 2013 in detail—what it is and how and why lesbian, gay, bisexual, and transgender (LGBT) people and others want to change the United States (and the world). It is a comprehensive guidebook for LGBT legal equality in America.

What legislation would need to be added or modified to reach equal treatment under the law? How do we go about doing it?

This book also shows the paths to equality, and it is an urgent call for action.

Part I describes what LGBT means and the arguments used to deny equal treatment under the law to this group of people.

Part II shows what the gay agenda is in detail, including the goals to be achieved.

Part III describes the different paths available to achieve equality.

Part IV is a call to action about what you can do in 2013 to achieve legal equality for the LGBT community.

Finally, the epilogue describes the ultimate goal—beyond legal equality.

What We Accomplished in 2012

Through the efforts of thousands of individuals, some acting on their own while some as parts of groups and organizations, legal equality for lesbian, gay, bisexual, and transgender (LGBT) Americans advanced very significantly in 2012:

- President Obama came out in favor of the freedom to marry the person you love.

- LGBT voters voted 76 percent for Obama versus 22 percent for Romney. This disparity, with the support of other minority voters, gave Obama the victory in states like Florida and Ohio.

- The people of Maryland voted to allow same-gender couples to get married.

- The people of Washington State voted for the same right for its residents.

- So did the people in Maine, for a total of nine states plus the District of Columbia that currently support same-gender marriage.

- The people of Minnesota voted down a constitutional amendment that would have enshrined discrimination in their state constitution by limiting marriage to different-gender couples. In an unprecedented win, the four ballot initiatives regarding marriage were won by the supporters of equality.

- The people of Wisconsin elected Tammy Baldwin to the US Senate, the first openly LGBT person in that position.

- The people of Colorado, Rhode Island, Arizona, New York, California, and Wisconsin elected openly LGB people to represent them in the US House of Representatives. With a total of six LGB representatives, this is an all-time record. For the first time, an openly bisexual person, Kyrsten

Sinema was elected to Congress representing Arizona—alas, no transgender member of Congress yet.

- For the first time in seven state legislatures, the people elected an openly LGBT person to represent them. In addition, the Washington senate elected Ed Murray (who is openly gay) as its majority leader. Moreover, the Colorado House of Representatives elected Mark Ferrandino (who is openly gay) as its speaker, and Oregon's House voted Tine Kotek (who is openly lesbian) as its speaker. They joined Gordon Fox, who has been the openly gay speaker of Rhode Island's House of Representatives since 2010.

- The Equal Employment Opportunity Commission ruled unanimously that transgender people are protected against employment discrimination under Title VII of the Civil Rights Act. Several other court rulings and agency rulings advanced employment nondiscrimination for transgender people, including protection under the Fourteenth Amendment to the US Constitution.

- Finally, in December 2012, the American Psychiatric Association removed gender identity disorder as a mental disease.

These unprecedented victories provide great momentum for a full-out action to finally achieve LGBT equality now.

Part I:

Who Are These LGBT People?

1.

Who Are These Lesbian, Gay, Bisexual, and Transgender (LGBT) People?

They are your neighbors, your coworkers, your elected officials (even if you may not realize it), your children or grandchildren (even if they do not know it yet). They are a small part of the population, but they are everywhere—in every culture, religion, location, and profession. Some live as couples, some as singles, and some are married to somebody of the opposite gender. What they all have in common is that their sexual orientation or gender identity or how they express their gender is different from the majority.

Some are exclusively attracted to members of the same gender. Others are attracted to both genders. Others feel that their anatomical gender of birth do not correspond to the gender their minds tell them they belong to. We call these people *LGBT* as the abbreviation for *lesbian, gay, bisexual, and transgender*.

Other people prefer to call themselves *queer*, which is an all-encompassing term for anybody who does not want to be classified as heterosexual or gay or lesbian or bisexual or transgender or any of the other classifications that are commonly in use. So, sometimes the term LGBTQ is also used to include *queer*. Also, the Q in LGBTQ can mean questioning, to represent people who are questioning their heterosexuality.

There are also people who are intersex, meaning that, from birth, they have both male and female genital characteristics. So another term in use is LGBTQIA for *lesbian, gay, bisexual, transexual, queer or questioning, intersex, and ally*.

There is also the term *two spirits*, used by Native Americans. Several books have been written on the topic.

Here is another, more recent term: *metrosexual*. It describes mostly men who are hip, cool, and fashionable. They are very comfortable with people of a different sexual orientation and gender identity. Metrosexuals themselves can be of any sexual orientation or gender identity or expression, although most are heterosexual.

By now, you may think that this book is *not* for you, since you may be more interested in issues such as:

- Why can't everybody just get along, marry somebody of the opposite sex, have children, and be productive members of society?

- What type of a country are we building in the United States if we allow the collapse of the traditional family?

- What type of a country are we building if we abandon our bedrock principles of individuality, respect for religion, separation of religion from state, and separation of powers in the three government branches?

This book answers these important questions. To have an opinion is easy. To learn the facts and be open to modifying our opinions based on new information is harder. Hopefully, you are willing to read here about other points of view that, you may be surprised to discover, are closer to your opinions than you may think.

Let's start with some fundamentals.

The gay agenda is not only about lesbian, gay, bisexual, and transgender people (LGBT). It is about *every person* because each of us has a sexual orientation and a gender identity and expression. As uncomfortable as the topic may be to some people, it is a very important component of who we are as people. Notice that sexual orientation refers to heterosexuality, homosexuality, and bisexuality. So laws and rules that apply to sexual orientation protect *every* person, *including heterosexuals.*

The American Psychological Association (apa.org/helpcenter/sexual-orientation.aspx) defines sexual orientation as follows:

> Sexual orientation refers to an enduring pattern of emotional, romantic, and/or sexual attractions to

men, women, or both sexes. Sexual orientation also refers to a person's sense of identity based on those attractions, related behaviors, and membership in a community of others who share those attractions.

Besides sexual orientation, we need to understand gender identity and expression, which is defined by the American Psychological Association (apa.org/topics/sexuality/transgender.aspx) as follows:

Gender identity refers to a person's internal sense of being male, female, or something else; gender expression refers to the way a person communicates gender identity to others through behavior, clothing, hairstyles, voice, or body characteristics.

Like sexual orientation, gender identity affects every person. Most people feel comfortable that their gender at birth match the gender that they feel they belong to. But some people feel differently. Some like to cross-dress, which is independent of sexual orientation (in fact, most cross-dressers are heterosexual—many in happy marriages). Others feel that they need to change their gender to the one they feel is their true gender.

Note that sexual orientation (the people to whom you are attracted) is different from gender identity (the gender to which you belong in your mind) and different from the expression of that gender. For instance, a male may have surgery to become a female (her gender identity is female) but at the same time be attracted to males (so her sexual orientation is heterosexual). In another example, a heterosexual female may like to dress manlier, so the gender expression may be that of a man despite that she is a heterosexual female. All the potential combinations can be mind-boggling the first time you hear about them, but life is complex and not just black and white.

For whatever reason, some people cannot comprehend why transgender people need to change the gender of birth. However, America has a proud tradition of commitment to freedom, happiness, and individuality, so respect for others' freedom, especially about private personal matters, will eventually prevail.

Before we continue with the rest of the book, it is very important to understand that people who are gay or lesbian or bisexual or transgender are not weirdos. In fact, many of them have made very important contributions to society. Appendix 1 lists many of them. The next chapter talks about everyday life.

2.

A Day in the Life of a Family

The alarm goes off. It is 6:00 a.m. It seems that the alarm always goes off too early.

Lisa drags herself out of bed. She barely makes it to the kitchen, where the coffee is already brewing. Ah! What technology can do! You set it up the night before, and coffee is ready when you wake up.

Thanks to the coffee, Lisa makes it to the shower then wakes up the kids and prepares breakfast.

Mornings are always such a struggle. It is never easy with four children: Michael, Danielle, David, and Katie. Rush, rush, and rush. Lisa takes the kids to the school bus. Today is going to be a tough day. Katie, the youngest of the couple's children, is home with the flu.

The couple adopted their four children. Nobody wanted these children because they all have special needs: drug exposure during pregnancy or HIV exposure in the womb or development delays. They are great kids, but, through no fault of their own, they were rejected by other adoptive parents. Fortunately, the two kids who were exposed to HIV in the womb have tested negative. Things are going well.

The rest of the morning flies by with going to the supermarket, taking care of Katie, and doing three loads of laundry.

In the afternoon, Lisa takes the kids to after-school activities. Lisa is a very busy stay-at-home mom. She teaches the first communion classes in her church. She is also the volunteer coordinator for her children's elementary school. And she also started two Girl Scout troops.

She is the supermom that even teenagers are proud of.

Lisa rushes home to prepare dinner. Just after 7:00 p.m., Janice, her partner of eighteen years, gets home. She is exhausted after a full day of work as a manager of a state child welfare program. She is well respected for her work and knowledge (with a master's in public administration and a master's in social work).

The conversation at the dinner table centers on the children. It always does. Lisa and Janice ask them how their day at school was, review their homework, and so on—the usual stuff.

By midnight, they both have fallen asleep on the couch, pretending to watch TV.

They feel blessed for what they have. Tomorrow surely the alarm will go off again at 6:00 a.m.

For these two moms, life is not different from that of any other family with children.

Or so they thought.

3.

A Bad Day in the Life of a Family

Lisa and Janice—along with their three youngest children, Danielle, David, and Katie—flew from rainy western Washington to sunny Florida to board a family cruise to the Bahamas to celebrate the couple's anniversary.

This was a trip that the children (and their parents) had so much looked forward to. They were in line early to board the ship. They had lunch together just after 1:00 p.m. Everyone was excited about relaxing together for an entire week as a family. What a great adventure awaited them!

After lunch, the children asked impatiently to explore the ship and headed to the top deck, where they found a basketball court. A court on a cruise ship—what could be cooler?

Janice said she was going to unpack and take a siesta (nothing like taking on a Latin tradition while in Miami). The ship wasn't scheduled to depart until 3:00 p.m., so there was plenty of time before the sail-away party.

Lisa, never one to sit still, joined the children on the top deck with her coffee in one hand and a camera in the other, not different from what any mother would do. It was such a happy day.

While taking pictures of the children, Lisa suddenly collapsed on the basketball court, spilling her coffee and dropping the camera. The children, just nine years to twelve years old, helped pick up their mom and navigated their way down ten decks to find their cabin to bang on the door and wake up their other mom, Janice.

With the help of Janice, they flagged down a porter to get a wheelchair since Lisa was unable to stand on her own. The family headed immediately to the medical center onboard. The doctor established that Lisa was gravely ill. He then requested the ship's captain to delay departure and ordered an urgent transfer to the trauma center in Miami at Jackson Memorial Hospital. Medics arrived to take over emergency care of Lisa while a sheriff's deputy escorted Janice, the children, and their luggage to a waiting taxi. The taxi and medics carrying Lisa arrived at Ryder Trauma Center almost simultaneously around three-thirty in the afternoon.

Janice attempted to follow the gurney carrying Lisa through the emergency entrance but was asked to go to the waiting room and speak with the clerk. Janice settled the children in some chairs and headed to the desk to speak with the clerk. She asked to fill out admitting papers for Lisa, her partner, but was told to "take a seat" and wait for someone to come speak with her.

Some time later, a man appeared and introduced himself as Garnett Frederick, a hospital social worker. He then informed Janice that she and her family were in an "antigay city and state," and that if Janice wanted to find out about Lisa's condition or even see her, she needed a healthcare proxy. He turned to leave, but Janice immediately asked for his fax number and informed him that he would get the documents.

Do you know of any couple who travels with a healthcare proxy? If Janice and Lisa were a man and a woman, would anybody have asked for any documents? Would anybody have to ask, even if the couple were not married, to be allowed in the room with each other?

Janice and Lisa had their healthcare power of attorney, living wills, and advanced directives documents drawn up in 2001, shortly after Janice was diagnosed with multiple sclerosis. They tucked the documents away, never envisioning they would need them until they were much older. On that day, Lisa was only thirty-nine years old. Janice, a trained trauma and emergency department social worker, ensured that the couple kept their healthcare proxy and decision-making documents up to date.

Janice wondered in that moment at Ryder Trauma center why their love and commitment of eighteen years was not recognized. With no time to think about such injustice, she jumped into action and called a trusted friend, who rushed to the couple's house, faxed the decision-making documents to Ryder Trauma Center, and called Janice just after 4:20 p.m. to check that the fax was received at the hospital—just forty minutes after Lisa's arrival from the ship.

All of Janice's pleas to find out Lisa's condition or to speak to medical personnel went unanswered despite that the hospital had received the healthcare power of attorney. Janice watched as other families, some with young children, were escorted back through locked doors to see their loved ones while Janice's and their children's anguish increased with every minute that passed.

With papers in hand, Janice would be informed, one would think, of Lisa's medical condition, even in an antigay city and state. At 6:00 p.m.—two and half hours after their arrival—Janice was faced with a decision that would change their family forever. Surgeons informed her that Lisa was nearly brain dead and they needed to know if they should proceed with surgery. Even if Lisa survived the surgery, she would live in a persistent vegetative state. Without even seeing her, Janice was forced to make the decision to follow Lisa's wishes of donating her organs. After the surgeons left, Janice was alone to tell the children that their other mom was going to heaven.

Over the next five and a half hours, Janice begged and pleaded to see Lisa and bring their children to the room to say goodbye. She resorted to showing the children's birth certificates, which listed both of them as mothers, to the desk clerk in an attempt to establish that the children were in fact Lisa's children. They were still not allowed to see their mother.

Janice requested a Catholic priest to administer Lisa's last rites. It was only then that she was given one opportunity to see Lisa for only five minutes.

After 11:30 p.m., when Janice and the children had waited eight hours in the hospital waiting room, Lisa's sister arrived after driving from her home in Jacksonville, Florida. Janice led Lisa's sister inside and brought her to the same desk clerk who worked there all night. Lisa's sister simply stated, "I'm Lisa Pond's sister, and I am here to see her." She was informed that Lisa was moved an hour earlier to the neuro ICU and was given the room number. Lisa's sister was not asked for identification or any paperwork proving her family relationship.

Lisa Pond died of a brain aneurysm at age thirty-nine on February 19, 2007, in Jackson Memorial Hospital. Her children and the love of her life, Janice Langbehn, were a few feet away—but in another room without being able to be with Lisa in her final moments.

Without being able to touch her. Without being able to kiss her goodbye. Without being able to say, "I love you" for the final time.

This is a true story. All the information is factual. That this cruel story happened in Miami, a city that has prospered from gay tourism, tells you that it can happen anywhere.

Janice Langbehn sued the hospital. The judge dismissed the case, despite stating that the hospital "exhibited a lack of compassion and was unbecoming of a renowned trauma center like Ryder [Jackson Memorial Hospital Trauma Center]. Unfortunately, no relief is available for these failures based on the allegations pleaded in the amended complaint."

In other words, there was nothing to sue about because no law had been broken. Hospital visitation discrimination like this was allowed in Florida and other states until January 18, 2011, when new regulations came into effect at the urging of President Obama after learning of the Langbehn-Pond story.

Lisa and Janice, together for eighteen years, parents of four children whom nobody else wanted, were cruelly denied a basic human need: to have your loved ones next to you when you die. In Janice's words, "Holding Lisa's hand is not a *gay* right but a *human* right."

4.

Your Family's Values

Family is very personal, and how you raise your family is up to you. As a father and mother said: "We don't want others to impose *their* family values on our family."

It is all about *your family's* values. For example, this father and mother's family values are clear: they have two daughters, Jackie and Debbie. One daughter is lesbian; the other is not. Taking turns, the parents both said, "Our family's values are that we treat our two daughters the same. We teach them the same ethics and values. We want them to have the same opportunities. We want them to be happy in their lives and one day to marry someone they love and start their own families. We treat our two daughters equally and expect the government to do the same. These are our family's values."

One day recently, this family found out that they held a prejudice that they had not previously realized. They encouraged their non-lesbian daughter, Jackie, to bring her boyfriend home for dinner (but not stay overnight) to ensure that he could get to know the family and vice versa. However, they were uncomfortable asking Debbie to bring her girlfriend.

The parents said: "We did not realize that we were treating our two daughters differently and that we could cause harm that way. Now we check everything we do as parents, to show both our daughters that we love them equally and unconditionally. And it is fine for our daughter Debbie to bring her girlfriend for dinner and family outings—but neither of our daughters gets to bring a boyfriend or girlfriend overnight." The parents and daughters laughed together as they recounted the story.

What this father and mother are doing is very good parenting. Scientific research by the Family Acceptance Project of San Francisco State University (familyproject.sfsu.edu) shows the following:

- Suicide attempts by LGBT youth who have high rejection from their family are more than *eight times* the attempts in families with low rejection for their LGBT children.

- Illegal drug use by LGBT youth who experience high rejection from their family is more than *three times* the use for those in families with low rejection for their LGBT children.

- Similarly, the risk of HIV infection is more than *three times* for LGBT youth in families with a high rejection for them.

- Yet another important statistic: 92 percent of LGBT youth in a family that is highly accepting believe that they can be a happy LGBT adult, while only 35 percent of those in a family that is not accepting believe it so.

Several religious leaders are working with the Family Acceptance Project because these scientific findings have opened their minds that tough love can be very detrimental to the health (and survival) of young LGBT people.

Each family member is entitled to his or her faith. You may believe that LGBT people will not go to heaven. Other family members may believe in an all-loving God and that a good person (whether gay or non-gay) will go to heaven. Every parent knows that *love for a child must be unconditional*, in good times and in bad.

There are several parental behaviors that increase the risk of LGBT children developing health and mental problems. These parental behaviors are determined to be unhealthy based not on opinion but on scientific research by the Family Acceptance Project (familyproject.sfsu.edu). Here are nine behaviors to avoid:

1. "Hitting, slapping or physically hurting your child because of their LGBT identity."

2. "Verbal harassment or name-calling because of your child's LGBT identity."

3. "Excluding LGBT youth from family and family identity."

4. "Blocking access to LGBT friends, events and resources."

5. "Blaming your child when they are discriminated against because of their LGBT identity."

6. "Pressuring your child to be more (or less) masculine or feminine."

7. "Telling your children that God will punish them because they are gay."

8. "Telling your child that you are ashamed of them or that how they look or act will shame the family."

9. "Making your child keep their LGBT identity a secret in the family and not letting them talk about it."

You determine your family's values. All parents want the best for their children. When parents decide what's best for their children, they draw on experiences with their parents (good or bad) and all the other experiences from which they have learned throughout their lives. However, most parents have no experience dealing with LGBT children. Fortunately, research conducted by the Family Acceptance Project shows parental behaviors that can be most helpful to their LGBT children. These recommendations are not based on opinions or beliefs but on research. Here are eleven things to do:

1. "Talk with your child or foster child about their LGBT identity."

2. "Express affection when your child tells you or when you learn that your child is gay or transgender."

3. "Support your child's LGBT identity even though you may feel uncomfortable."

4. "Advocate for your child when he or she is mistreated because of their LGBT identity."

5. "Require that other family members respect your LGBT child."

6. "Bring your child to LGBT organizations or events."

7. "Talk with your clergy and help your faith community to support LGBT people."

8. "Connect your child with an LGBT adult role model to show them options for the future."

9. "Welcome your child's LGBT friends and partners to your home."

10. "Support your child's gender expression."

11. "Believe your child can have a happy future as an LGBT adult."

This scientific research is opening up many minds—teaching parents to understand the unintended consequences of their past behavior.

For religious parents, this may appear like a conflict, especially when some churches say that homosexuality is an abomination. However, more and more religious leaders are reaching out after understanding the science—and more and more Christian parents accept what Jesus has always taught: unconditional love and commitment, not tough love but *unconditional love and commitment*, which is the basis of marriage and of having children. Good parents always want to protect their children from harm.

The father and mother in this story concluded by saying:

> In our family we do not value treating one child differently from the other. We value, cherish, and celebrate their uniqueness because each of our children is a gift.

You determine your family's values.

What, then, is the definition of a family?

5.

Defining *Family*

In the last few chapters we have met two families: one a nontraditional but sanctified union, the other with more traditional parents but daughters of different sexual orientations.

How *does* one then define a family? Traditionalists have a clear answer: mother + father + children. This is *their* definition of family. What's *your* definition for *your* family?

As an example, here is the definition that Baptist Health South Florida has for a family (in their 2011 *Outcomes*—a compilation of articles from their Center for Performance Excellence):

> The word *family* triggers images of different "support groups" for each of us. Over time, the "social support group" to us changes, shifts, or expands throughout our lives.
>
> At Baptist Health, each patient defines those individuals who are most important to them—who they view as "family." We recognize and value the importance of these individuals in the healing process. These people may include, but are not limited to, family, friends, and/or other support persons, such as a spouse, a domestic partner (including same-sex domestic partner), other relatives, neighbors, coworkers or clergy. **In other words, each patient has the right to define who can be present and participate in their care and visitation.**

The bold typeface is in the original article. Note that Baptist Health South Florida is a *faith-based* healthcare organization ranking at the top in the United States. They understand the definition of a family since they see patients constantly defining who their families are.

Each of us knows who our true family is: the people we turn to when we are most in need. How have we come to allow others to impose a definition of who should be our families?

This is an attack on our personal freedom.

People use several arguments to deny others' freedoms. Let's examine these arguments one by one in the next chapters.

6.

It's Unnatural!

Some people think that homosexual, bisexual, and transgender people are mentally sick, that what they do is unnatural, and that the Bible says it is an abomination. These beliefs serve as a justification for people to discriminate, such as to deny a family the right to be together when the mother is dying at a public hospital, as we saw in Chapter 3.

Would God accept the behavior of the people in that hospital in Miami who did not allow Lisa's partner to be next to her as she was dying? What about their young children, who had nothing to do with their parents' sexual orientation?

Let's discuss now one of the most common arguments used to discriminate: that homosexuality is a sin against nature.

To see if it is true, we need to check whether homosexuality and bisexuality exist in animals in nature.

Evidence is very clear that many animals exhibit homosexual and bisexual behaviors. Here are just a few examples from Wikipedia (en.wikipedia.org/wiki/Homosexual_behavior_in_animals):

- *Giraffes:* about nine out of ten matings occur between males.

- *Domesticated sheep:* about 10 percent of males do not mate with females—only males.

- *Black swans:* about 25 percent of the matings are between males. Male couples also raise young black swans.

- *Western gulls:* 10 to 15 percent of females show homosexual behavior.

- *Wild ducks:* about 19 percent of all pairings are male with male.

- *Penguins:* many male-to-male long-term relationships have been reported, including building nests together.

- *Vultures:* bisexual vultures have been studied in zoos.

- *Pigeons:* male-male and female-female relationships have been documented. Same-gender couples build nests together.

- *American bisons:* same-sex relationships are documented as common.

- *Bonobos (apes):* they are considered a bisexual species (60 percent of sexual activity is between two or more females).

- *Dolphins:* there is well-reported bisexual behavior, especially among bottlenose dolphins.

- *Elephants:* there is well-documented bisexual behavior, with stronger bonds between males.

- *Lions:* about 8 percent of mountings are male-male.

- *Spotted hyena:* have strong female-to-female relationships.

- *Lizards:* females can take masculine or feminine sexual roles.

- *Dragonflies:* high incidence of mating among males.

This article concludes, *"No species has been found in which homosexual behavior has not been shown to exist, except for species that never have sex at all."* Therefore, we cannot say that homosexuality and bisexuality are unnatural when they have been well-documented in nature.

Some people would say, "Fine, we cannot say that it is unnatural, but these people are mentally sick." The next chapter responds to this pronouncement.

7.

You Are Sick!

Given the scientific evidence, we need to agree that homosexuality and bisexuality occur naturally in animals. What about in humans? Has this topic been studied by science? The answer is yes. Research by psychologists like Alfred Kinsey, Magnus Hirschfeld, and Sigmund Freud, among others, shows that sexual orientation appears as a spectrum from totally heterosexual to bisexual to totally homosexual.

Repeated studies show that people fall into different parts of the spectrum of sexual orientation. This is a natural phenomenon. For example, handedness falls also into a continuous spectrum: most people are right-handed, some are left-handed, and some are ambidextrous.

The American Psychological Association confirms:
(www.apa.org/helpcenter/sexual-orientation.aspx)

> Both heterosexual behavior and homosexual behavior are normal aspects of human sexuality. Both have been documented in many different cultures and historical eras. Despite the persistence of stereotypes that portray lesbian, gay, and bisexual people as disturbed, several decades of research and clinical experience have led all mainstream medical and mental health organizations in this country to conclude that these orientations represent normal forms of human experience. Lesbian, gay, and bisexual relationships are normal forms of human bonding. Therefore, these mainstream organizations long ago abandoned classifications of homosexuality as a mental disorder.

Clearly, scientific organizations have concluded that homosexuality, heterosexuality, and bisexuality are normal forms of the human experience and that they are not mental disorders.

We cannot say that homosexuality is unnatural since it occurs in nature. Furthermore, we cannot say that people with a homosexual sexual orientation are sick since it has been proven scientifically not to be the case.

But, you may say, the Bible says homosexuality is an abomination. You are right on this one—read on.

8.

The Bible Says So

We have already seen that we cannot call homosexuality unnatural since it is well-documented that it happens in nature. Nor can we say that homosexuality is a disease since for many years the American Psychological Association and other organizations have clearly stated that it is a normal aspect of human sexuality.

So, it's not unnatural, and it is not a disease. However, some people believe that, based on what the Bible says, homosexuality is an abomination.

Indeed, Leviticus 18:22 (King James Version) clearly says, "Thou shalt not lie with mankind, as with womankind: it is an abomination." Some experts contend that the term *abomination* is mistranslated. But since religion is based on personal faith, we should respect those who take the meaning literally.

Furthermore, Leviticus 20:13 (King James Version) establishes the death penalty for homosexual acts:

> If a man also lie with mankind, as he lieth with a woman, both of them have committed an abomination: they shall surely be put to death; their blood shall be upon them.

If you are willing to accept that homosexual acts are an abomination subject to the death penalty then you have to accept the penalty that the same chapter of Leviticus establishes:

> **Leviticus 20:9** For every one that curseth his father or his mother shall be surely put to death: he hath cursed his father or his mother; his blood shall be upon him.

> **Leviticus 20:10** And the man that committeth adultery with another man's wife, even he that committeth adultery with his neighbour's wife, the

adulterer and the adulteress shall surely be put to death.

Leviticus 20:11 And the man that lieth with his father's wife hath uncovered his father's nakedness: both of them shall surely be put to death; their blood shall be upon them.

Leviticus 20:12 And if a man lie with his daughter in law, both of them shall surely be put to death: they have wrought confusion; their blood shall be upon them.

Leviticus 20:13 If a man also lie with mankind, as he lieth with a woman, both of them have committed an abomination: they shall surely be put to death; their blood shall be upon them.

Leviticus 20:14 And if a man take a wife and her mother, it is wickedness: they shall be burnt with fire, both he and they; that there be no wickedness among you.

Leviticus 20:15 And if a man lie with a beast, he shall surely be put to death: and ye shall slay the beast.

Leviticus 20:16 And if a woman approach unto any beast, and lie down thereto, thou shalt kill the woman, and the beast: they shall surely be put to death; their blood shall be upon them.

Leviticus 20:17 And if a man shall take his sister, his father's daughter, or his mother's daughter, and see her nakedness, and she see his nakedness; it is a wicked thing; and they shall be cut off in the sight of their people: he hath uncovered his sister's nakedness; he shall bear his iniquity.

Leviticus 20:18 And if a man shall lie with a woman having her sickness, and shall uncover her nakedness; he hath discovered her fountain, and she hath uncovered the fountain of her blood: and both of them shall be cut off from among their people.

Leviticus 20:19 And thou shalt not uncover the nakedness of thy mother's sister, nor of thy father's sister: for he uncovereth his near kin: they shall bear their iniquity.

Leviticus 20:20 And if a man shall lie with his uncle's wife, he hath uncovered his uncle's nakedness: they shall bear their sin; they shall die childless.

Leviticus 20:21 And if a man shall take his brother's wife, it is an unclean thing: he hath uncovered his brother's nakedness; they shall be childless.

So if you curse your father or mother, you should be put to death. And if you commit adultery with a married woman, both of you should be put to death. So if you accept that homosexual acts are an abomination that results in the perpetrators deserving to be put to death then you should be consistent with the other commandments in the same chapter of Leviticus. There are more commandments in Leviticus:

Leviticus 11:10−12 And all that have not fins and scales in the seas, and in the rivers, of all that move in the waters, and of any living thing which is in the waters, they shall be an abomination unto you. They shall be even an abomination unto you; ye shall not eat of their flesh, but ye shall have their carcasses in abomination. Whatsoever hath no fins nor scales in the waters, that shall be an abomination unto you.

So, not only are homosexual acts an abomination but eating shrimp and other fish without fins is an abomination, too. The point is not to debate or contest *your* interpretation of the Bible. Some Christians believe that the translation may not consider the context of the times and the exact meaning of the words. Other Christians believe that the Bible should be read literally; if this is your belief, please act consistently by choosing what you cannot eat and lobby to establish the death penalty not only for homosexual acts but also for the heterosexual acts listed in Leviticus. The point here is not to change your religious beliefs but to encourage you to be *consistent* with them. In fact, it is very important to respect and protect the freedom of religion, as the next chapter attests.

9.

Your Freedom of Religion

Clearly, in a civilized society, we are not going to execute men who commit adultery with married women, just as we are not going to execute people who have romantic relationships with a person of the same gender. Similarly, in a civilized society, we are not going to call people with a homosexual sexual orientation an abomination but remain silent about people who commit the abomination, per Leviticus 11, of eating shrimp or any shellfish.

Fortunately, most Americans want to respect each other's freedom of religion. It is true: some religions do believe that homosexual acts should be penalized and that indeed people with a homosexual sexual orientation should not be treated equally under the law. However, some other religions differ; they believe that every person is a child of God, loved by God, and should be treated equally.

Some people, however, work hard to attack the freedom of religion. In January 2013, the National Cathedral, which is the second largest church in the United States and part of the Episcopal faith, announced that it will marry people of the same gender. A month after that decision, the Faith and Freedom Coalition, an organization founded by conservative Ralph Reed, demanded "an immediate suspension of any current or future federal funds to this institution." So much for their belief in freedom of religion.

How do we go about protecting freedom of religion?

We should protect the freedom of each religion, since we can only protect your freedom of religion if we protect others' freedom of religion. If your religion believes that homosexuality is an abomination and does not allow people of the same gender to marry, it is fine. If your religion accepts people with a homosexual sexual orientation and their right to marry, fine, too. The government should not impose on any religion whom to marry (or divorce) or force any religion to have bishops who are female or LGBT.

Government cannot impose one religion's views on another. This is why each religion is regulated by its own laws and civic life by its own laws. Americans cherish the requirement expressed in the United States Constitution:

> Congress shall make no law respecting an establishment of religion, or prohibiting the free exercise thereoff.

The greatness of our country comes from not allowing Sharia law to control all of us. Nor do we allow Jewish law, or Catholic law, or Baptist law to control all of us. Every individual is free to follow the law of his or her church, while the government creates and enforces civil law.

Still, some people say that our *civil* laws should not treat people with a homosexual sexual orientation equally because homosexuality is a choice. But is it a choice? The next chapter tackles this important question.

10.

Is Homosexuality a Choice?

Sexual orientation defines our attraction to other people. By definition, sexual orientation can be heterosexual (attracted to people of a different gender), homosexual (attracted to people of the same gender), or bisexual (attracted to people of either gender).

So the question is: is sexual orientation a choice?

Ask this question to yourself. Is *your* sexual orientation a choice? If you answer yes, when did you choose your sexual orientation? How did you make that choice?

Or, more pointedly, for heterosexuals: when did you decide to be a heterosexual? Did you decide you were heterosexual even before you had sex? Did you always know because you were just born that way? Did it just come naturally?

Certainly, most readers have answered no—meaning that sexual orientation was not a choice for them. Bisexual individuals may answer that at some point they were attracted to one gender and at some other point in their lives to the other or that they were equally attracted to both.

If your child tells you that he or she is gay or lesbian or bisexual or transgender, do not blame yourself. *You did nothing wrong.* You did not influence him or her to be LGBT, nor did your parents influence you to be a heterosexual, just as homosexual parents cannot influence their children to be LGBT. It is the way it is. There is growing research that the sexual orientation of the parents—heterosexual, homosexual, or bisexual—does not affect the orientation of the children they raise.

The people who believe that homosexuality is a choice use this to deny people with a different sexual orientation or gender identity equal protection under the law. They claim that the law should protect all citizens equally regardless of race, gender, or national origin because those factors are obviously not a choice.

Here is the catch: while the law protects against discrimination based on non-choice characteristics such as race, gender, and national origin, it also protects *religion*—which is clearly a personal choice. So you cannot fairly say that it is okay to discriminate against gays because being gay is a choice. Even if homosexuality were a choice, it should be protected against discrimination.

There is yet another argument that some people still use to justify discrimination against gay, lesbian, bisexual, and transgender people. They say it can be cured. Let's consider this question in the next chapter.

11.

Let *Me* Straighten *You*

If your sexual orientation is heterosexual, do you think that with therapy you could become homosexual?

You are very likely to answer: *"No way. Nobody would be able to make me homosexual. And I do not want to change anyway."*

Indeed, most people do not want to change something as intrinsic as their sexual orientation, whether they are heterosexual, homosexual, or bisexual.

However, there is heavy societal pressure to belong to the majority. So whether because of their religion, or not knowing that sexual orientation fall naturally into a spectrum, or fear of rejection by society, some people still struggle with their sexual orientation. They try to change their sexual orientation to heterosexual and "be cured." Some families, for similar reasons, bring their children to therapy (called reparative or conversion therapy) to make them straight.

As hard as it might be to believe for those who think that homosexuality is an abomination, there is nothing to be cured.

The most important study on the subject was conducted in 2001 by Robert Spitzer, MD, a well-respected professor of psychiatry at Columbia University. Dr. Spitzer addressed the issue of whether individuals could change their sexual orientation from homosexual to heterosexual using reparative or conversation therapy. He concluded that *some* highly motivated individuals could do it. The report was published in the *Archives of Sexual Behavior* but was not peer-reviewed, a critical requirement for any scientific work. Eventually, Dr. Spitzer concluded that his research was fundamentally flawed, and that there was no evidence that reparative therapy worked because statements from participants about their self-evaluation of the success of such therapy could not be relied upon.

This is what the American Psychological Association has to say regarding therapies to change sexual orientation: (www.apa.org/helpcenter/sexual-orientation.aspx)

> To date, there has been no scientifically adequate research to show that therapy aimed at changing sexual orientation (sometimes called reparative or conversion therapy) is safe or effective. Furthermore, it seems likely that the promotion of change therapies reinforces stereotypes and contributes to a negative climate for lesbian, gay, and bisexual persons. This appears to be especially likely for lesbian, gay, and bisexual individuals who grow up in more conservative religious settings.

So there is no evidence that such therapies are safe or effective.

The most prominent organization involved in so-called reparative or conversion therapy is Exodus International. In an interesting twist, Michael Bussee, one of its cofounders, left the organization in 1979 to live together with another cofounder of Exodus, Gary Cooper. To go even further, they had a commitment ceremony in 1982 (well before civil unions or marriage equality existed).

Years later, in October 2000, the chair of Exodus International, John Paulk, was removed from his position after being spotted drinking and flirting at a gay bar in Washington, DC.

More recently, in 2011, John Smid, the former executive director of Love in Action (another organization that claimed to "straighten homosexuals"), said, "I never met a man who experienced a change from homosexual to heterosexual."

Putting a final nail to this coffin, Alan Chambers, the president of Exodus International, said in June 2012 that "there was no cure for homosexuality and that 'reparative therapy' offered false hopes to gays and could even be harmful."

So it doesn't work.

Another organization that tries to straighten LGBT people is Courage, a Catholic apostolate. There's a twist: Paul Scalia, a priest who is the son of virulently antigay Supreme Court Justice Scalia, works there.

A very good resource and an organization worth supporting is Truth Wins Out (thruthwinsout.org). This organization specializes in debunking the ex-gay myth and counters disinformation campaigns about LGBT people. Its founder, Wayne Besen, is the author of *Anything but Straight: Unmasking the Scandals and Lies Behind the Ex-Gay Myth*. It is a book worth reading if you want to know more about this topic.

Some people may say, "Okay, I accept gays but please do not flaunt it." This concern is addressed in the following chapter.

12.

Don't Flaunt It

Some people say they can *tolerate* people who are gay, lesbian, bisexual, or transgender—but they add: "Just don't flaunt it." These people think that not "flaunting" sexual orientation, or hiding it, is a good compromise. In reality, this so-called compromise is harming (albeit unintentionally) LGBT people.

An important part of a healthy mind is to be able to be who you are. This was a main argument expressed by the chairman of the Joint Chiefs of Staff, Admiral Mullen, in support of the repeal of "Don't Ask, Don't Tell": it is *immoral* to force people to lie about and hide who they are.

Furthermore, a civilized society means that we respect other people—not just tolerate them. For instance, many years ago, the World Jewish Congress changed its vocabulary from "tolerance" to "respect."

It is wonderful to see a couple holding hands and showing their love. It is a public demonstration of commitment, love, and caring. It is wonderful independent of the gender of the couple. Notice that we are talking about public displays of affection—not about having sex in public (which is not appropriate whether the couple is same gender or different gender).

But what about the children? Some people say, "I do not want my children to see a homosexual couple. It is bad for the kids." Some people say that out of concern that seeing such a couple will make the child homosexual. Of course, this is not true: if you are heterosexual, can you fathom for a second that you would have become homosexual just by seeing a same-gender couple holding hands when you were a child? Let's be real.

In reality, you may be causing harm to your children if they see you reacting negatively about a same-gender couple's public display of affection. The message that you are sending is that homosexuality is wrong and that you may not love your children if they are homosexual. Seeing a same-gender public display of affection is an opportunity for you to teach the importance of understanding for, acceptance of, and respect for other human beings—and to let your children know that you will still love them even if they are homosexual or bisexual or transgender. Because you *will* still love them—won't you?

For those interested in the science, here is what the American Psychological Association has to say:
(www.apa.org/helpcenter/sexual-orientation.aspx)

> Sexual orientation is commonly discussed as if it were solely a characteristic of an individual, like biological sex, gender identity, or age. This perspective is incomplete because sexual orientation is defined in terms of relationships with others. People express their sexual orientation through behaviors with others, including such simple actions as holding hands or kissing. Thus, sexual orientation is closely tied to the intimate personal relationships that meet deeply felt needs for love, attachment, and intimacy. In addition to sexual behaviors, these bonds include nonsexual physical affection between partners, shared goals and values, mutual support, and ongoing commitment. Therefore, sexual orientation is not merely a personal characteristic within an individual. Rather, one's sexual orientation defines the group of people in which one is likely to find the satisfying and fulfilling romantic relationships that are an essential component of personal identity for many people.

So, it is about flaunting it. The freedom to be yourself is a part of one's sexual orientation and gender identity and expression and is a necessary component of a healthy lifestyle. It is about the freedom and respect to be yourself and have your individuality. Some people get it—check the next chapter.

13.

Understand, Accept, and Respect

More than thirty years ago, a young man, proud of being the big man in high school, started his first day of college to discover that he had been assigned a gay roommate. He was surprised but accepted it. After their freshman year, their lives took different courses. This young man ended up on Wall Street and was by the Twin Towers on September 11, 2001. Thankfully, he survived.

Life continued, and when President Obama announced his support for the freedom to marry, this young man e-mailed his freshman roommate of more than thirty years ago:

> With the President coming out and making a statement on same sex marriage I reference you often. I speak that you and I still stay in touch after all these years and that you were the first person to contact me after 9/11. I will always remember that. I have you and your friends to thank for enabling me to understand, accept and respect gay people. Being 18 and big man on campus in HS, if you were going to tell me that my college roommate would be gay, I would have said you're crazy. Just another example of not judging a book by its cover. It's wonderful that the time we were roommates has left a lasting impact on me.
>
> Thanks again.
>
> Be well.

Understand, accept, and respect.

That's all that needs to be said.

14.

It's about Personal Freedom; It's about Being Better People

The essence of personal freedom is to live and let live. For you to be free means that others need to be free. For example, you are free to follow a religious belief that homosexuality is an abomination. But you have to let others be free to follow their own religious belief that God loves all His creatures equally, including practicing homosexuals.

However, you are not free to cause bodily or psychological harm to others.

You should not stop others from having the same rights as you do or vote against them having the same rights that you have.

So this book is about freedom, as well as being better people.

It's about respecting others' choices—giving them freedom, even if we disagree. You may not want romantic intimacy with somebody of the same gender. However, we should respect and celebrate the fact that two people love each other—even if they are the same gender.

Being better people is about knowing that we are *not judging*. It is not about tolerating others but about respecting and celebrating their freedom to be unique—maybe very different from you or from the majority but still unique individuals with their virtues and faults, like each of us.

Being a better person, being free and respecting the personal freedom of others, and being treated equally under the law are the fundamental essence that most of us who love our country share.

15.

Summary: Who Are These LGBT People?

In the preceding chapters, we have learned a little bit more about lesbian, gay, bisexual, and transgender individuals. In summary, LGBT people are not alien to our lives. They are our neighbors, paramedics, firefighters, elected officials, military personnel, writers, police officers, and others in all professions, backgrounds, and locations. They are also people who have made very important contributions to society in the military, the sciences, the arts, and many other fields. We have seen that you cannot call homosexuality or bisexuality unnatural since it happens every day in nature. Science also agrees that homosexuality is not a disease and that there is nothing to cure, nor is there any effective method to change an individual's sexual orientation.

We have also seen that although the Bible can be interpreted as saying that homosexual acts are an abomination, not everybody agrees with that interpretation. (But if you do, to be consistent you cannot commit any other abomination, such as eating shrimp.)

Freedom of religion is very important. Since different religions have different religious laws about matters such as marriage, divorce, ordination, role of women, etc., we cannot impose one religion over another when we create *civil laws.*

Further, we've learned that the issue is not whether homosexuality is a choice: religion is clearly a personal choice and is included in all of our nondiscrimination legislation (as it should be).

Finally, we've seen that family values are defined by each family. For many families, a most important value is that they want all their children to be treated equally—independent of their sexual orientation or gender identity or expression.

Now that we know who these LGBT people are, it is time to examine the gay agenda. What do lesbian, gay, bisexual, and transgender individuals want? Do they want special rights? These and other questions will be explored in the next chapters.

Part II:

Why A Gay Agenda?

16.

Special Rights

Does anyone deserve special rights?

Think about it. Commit to an answer.

My answer is this: yes, some people deserve special rights.

What?

You got it right: some people do deserve special rights. Take, for example, a married couple. They get special rights. Here are some of the special rights married couples get:

- Unlimited, tax-free transfer of assets between spouses (including at death)

- Filing taxes jointly

- Making medical decisions for each other and their children

- Survivor Social Security benefits after death of a spouse

- Funeral and bereavement leave

- Ability to file wrongful death claims

- Spousal communications privilege that protects confidential communications between spouses during civil and criminal cases

- Spousal testimonial privilege that allows spouses not to testify against each other in a court of law

- Ability to sponsor the other spouse for immigration to the United States

- Joint adoption and foster care

- Automatic legal status with stepchildren

These are just some of the 1,138 special rights that married people get (per the report of the United States General Accounting Office dated January 23, 2004). Indeed, they should get them.

There are also special rights conferred to some people as protections against discrimination or hate crimes. These special rights are based on characteristics at birth that cannot be changed, such as race, gender, and country of origin. Some of the special protections are based on characteristics that are, and should be, a personal choice, such as choice of religion.

So, LGBT people are not seeking special rights that nobody else receives—just to be treated like people in the same circumstances.

If you are not gay, why should you care about gay rights? You might be surprised by some of the reasons, discussed in the following chapter.

17.

If I Am Not Gay, Why Should I Care about Gay Rights?

Because the crucial issue is not about gay rights; it is about who we are as a country and as good human beings. Do we accept the personal freedom of others to be unique individuals? Should anybody have to fear for their lives or their jobs just for being who they are? It is all about basic human rights. It is about the fundamental belief that we all share in America to be treated equally under the law.

Also, you should care if you have young children or grandchildren. They already have a sexual orientation (heterosexual, homosexual, or bisexual), even if they are too young to know. We have already discussed that conversion therapies do not work. Wouldn't you then want for them to live in a country in which they are treated equally under the law, independent of their sexual orientation and gender identity and expression?

Here's another example: say that you are heterosexual and a great accountant who wants to work for an LGBT organization that provides great benefits and it is close to your home. You should not be discriminated against because of your sexual orientation; you should be able to work for a gay organization. Discrimination based on sexual orientation (heterosexual, homosexual, or bisexual) should not be allowed, and the same goes for gender identity (the gender you identify with) and expression (how you express your gender).

Here's one more example: imagine you are outside a public restroom holding your wife's purse. You are 100-percent heterosexual, but some thugs think that because you are holding a purse, you are homosexual, and they attack you as they shout, "Faggot! Faggot! Here is what you deserve!" This is a true story.

Nobody deserves to be a victim of a hate crime. Thanks to legislation passed by Congress and signed into law in 2009 by

President Obama, you are protected against hate crimes because of your religion, race, national origin, gender, sexual orientation, gender identity and expression, and disability.

Now that you care about equal rights for everybody, what's the gay agenda? We'll get closer to an answer in the next chapter, which describes a gay congressman's agenda.

18.

Barney Frank's Radical Homosexual Agenda

Barney Frank was, until his retirement in January 2013, the most senior openly gay member of Congress. He was a member of Congress for more than thirty years and was chair of the powerful House Financial Services Committee for four years. He was considered by many to be a very savvy legislator. He is a graduate of Harvard College and Harvard Law School.

On December 22, 2010, four days after Congress repealed "Don't Ask, Don't Tell," Representative Frank addressed, during a press conference, what others called the "Barney Frank radical homosexual agenda." He said that this agenda was:

1. To be protected against violent crimes driven by bigotry

2. To be able to get married

3. To be able to get a job

4. To be able to fight for our country

He added, "For those who are worried about the radical homosexual agenda, let me put them on notice—two down, two to go." As for the "two down," he was referring to the repeal of "Don't Ask, Don't Tell" and the expansion of federal hate-crimes legislation to include sexual orientation and gender identity and expression. The "two to go" referred to the right to get married and to employment nondiscrimination.

As much as he is respected, and as much as his speech was wonderful and punchy, this is not the gay agenda. As the next chapter discusses, we need to think bigger.

19.

Thinking *Bigger*

Congressman Frank's "two down, two to go" should be more like "one and a half down, several more to go."

The "one" that is "down" is the hate-crimes protection that was achieved (at the federal level) when President Obama signed into law the Matthew Shepard and James Byrd, Jr. Hate Crimes Prevention Act on October 28, 2009. Here's a caveat: this legislation, while very useful, is not a replacement for state hate-crimes legislation, which is really needed in each state.

A goal that is half down is for service members serving openly in the military. As we explain in Chapter 27, these service members can still be discriminated against, and transgender service members are still not allowed to serve their country.

In terms of the two to go, Congressman Frank is referring to marriage and employment nondiscrimination. However, there are more than two goals that need to be achieved, including anti-bullying and safety in the schools, parenting rights, and nondiscrimination in housing, financing, public accommodations, and federal government programs.

The LGBT movement, while making significant progress (especially in the states, courts, and public opinion), suffers from not thinking big enough. We saw that Barney Frank's "radical homosexual agenda" was incomplete. For some people, the approach is: *ask for little—get even less.*

So, what's the real gay agenda? The true gay agenda is disclosed in detail in the next chapter.

20.

Q: What's the Gay Agenda?

A: The American Agenda: Equal Treatment under the Law

"The compelling argument is on the side of homosexuals. That's where the compelling argument is: 'We're Americans. We just want to be treated like everybody else.'"

—Bill O'Reilly on Fox News, March 26, 2013

The gay agenda is very simple: being treated equally under the law, which happens to be the American Agenda. This is the shared belief among Americans that has made us such a great country. It is the Golden Rule of treating others as you want to be treated.

To achieve the gay agenda, just look at the laws (federal and state) —whenever you see protections based on race, gender, national origin, and religion, just add the words *sexual orientation* and *gender identity*.

That's it. As Harvey Milk said:

> All men are created equal. No matter how hard you try, you can never erase those words.

If you have read the previous chapters of this book, you know that:

- Nobody is asking for special rights. LGBT people just want to be treated like other groups—no need to create special legislation for us. Just add "sexual orientation and gender identity" to existing legislation.

- Nobody is comparing the suffering of different groups protected under the law. People have suffered tremendous discrimination and prejudice because of their races. People have suffered tremendous discrimination and prejudice because of their gender, and because of their national origin, and because of their religion, and because of their sexual orientation, and because of their gender identity.

- Nobody wants to curtail your freedom of religion. Some religions support LGBT equality while others oppose it. The government cannot pick one religion over another. So public policy is based on treating everybody equally under the law. Each religion has the right to decide whom to marry, whom to allow to remarry in that faith, or whom to elevate to priesthood, among other rights.

- Whether being LGBT is a choice or not is irrelevant in this discussion. Religion clearly is a personal choice, and it is (and should be) protected against discrimination. Similarly, sexual orientation and gender identity and expression should be protected, too.

So what are the areas of the law in which LGBT people are not treated equally?

- Hates crimes
- Nondiscrimination
- Military
- Marriage equality
- Freedom of gender
- Protecting youth
- Same-gender parenting

Each of these areas is an equality goal—what needs to be achieved to be treated equally under the law. Each equality goal is discussed in detail in the successive chapters.

One point to note before we continue: some people can debate that the real gay agenda is social justice or to be equal in real life, not just under the law. This is a very honorable objective. However, as we have seen in prior chapters, real equality comes very slowly, even after legal equality is reached. For example, forty-five years after interracial marriage was made legal in all fifty states by the

Supreme Court, some people still oppose it (a significant number of people, in some states).

For the real, long-term gay agenda, do not miss reading the epilogue. The immediate focus of our energy is on legal equality under the law. How difficult is this to achieve?

21.

It's Not Rocket Science

Some problems are very difficult. Launching a rocket to the moon, landing it there, and bringing the astronauts safely home is a very difficult problem. We are the only country in the world to have solved it. Overhauling the medical system in a country is a difficult problem. Treating everybody equally under the law is not a difficult problem to solve. Here is how it can be done:

1. Examine the areas of the law in which lesbian, gay, bisexual, and transgender individuals are not treated equally. Call these areas equality goals. (This is simple, yet LGBT organizations still talk about issues instead of goals—just check their websites.)

2. Create a way to measure progress at the federal level and in each of the states so you can report accurately how many have been achieved instead of saying, "Two down, two to go," as Representative Frank claimed.

3. Write these equality goals in legal terms. You can put it all into an omnibus bill. Whether you seek passage as one bill or as a collection of bills is not as critical. An omnibus bill shows, in legal terms, what we need to achieve. It also shows that we are not seeking special rights because the main thing that we are doing is adding the terms *sexual orientation* and *gender identity* in places in current law that protect race, gender, national origin, and religion.

4. Identify the different paths that there are to achieve each goal: by the legislatures, by the courts, and by popular vote. Different people and different organizations will take different paths to achieve each of the equality goals. Insofar we agree on the goals, different paths are fine because it is very difficult to know in advance which path will lead us to equality faster.

5. Endorse candidates for elected office with clear criteria. A good endorsement process needs to result in more than just an endorse-or-don't-endorse outcome. It is also important to make the endorsement criteria public.

6. Check that endorsed candidates, once elected, sponsor and vote for equality legislation.

7. Legislate to cover *all* the members of the LGBT community.

Understanding what needs to be done is not rocket science. The following chapters examine each of the steps, starting with each of the equality goals to be achieved.

22.

Equality Goal: Nondiscrimination

Mary gets to work to find a note from her boss to see him immediately. Upon entering his office, she can tell that something is wrong.

The boss tells her that she is being fired. She says, "You mean laid off?" The boss says, "No, you are being fired—no layoff package, no unemployment benefits."

Mary is in shock. She thinks about the twelve years she has spent with the company in Florida. In her mind, she goes through the annual raises, the promotions, the wonderful reviews.

She tells the boss, "Tell it to me straight. Why am I getting fired?" The boss doesn't want to tell. Finally, having known Mary for so many years, he talks. The boss says, "My new boss told me that he doesn't want dykes working here."

Mary calls a friend who is an attorney. The attorney says, "I don't need to think about the case very much." Mary is intrigued. The attorney friend continues, "There is absolutely nothing that anyone can do."

Mary is confused. In her state of Florida, like in the majority of states, if the company would have dismissed her by saying that her performance was not good enough, she could have fought it in court by asking them to prove it—given that her annual performance reviews clearly said the contrary. However, because she was dismissed for being a lesbian, there is nothing that she can do. Sexual orientation and gender identity and expression are not protected in her state. Nor is it protected at the federal level.

Protection for sexual orientation also means protection if you are discriminated against for being heterosexual. Say that you are a bartender working in California in a gay bar and you get fired because you are heterosexual (this actually happened). Because California has a nondiscrimination statute that covers sexual orientation and gender identity and expression, the heterosexual bartender got his job back because you do not need to be gay to be a good bartender in a gay bar.

One of the groups that suffer the most discrimination is people whose gender do not match their gender at birth. Transgender people get severely discriminated against in employment, housing, access to public assistance, and so many aspects vital to everyday life. So it is absolutely critical that, when seeking equality under the law, we always include sexual orientation *and* gender identity and expression.

Fortunately, on April 20, 2012, the EEOC (Equal Employment Opportunity Commission), in a unanimous ruling, decided that transgender and gender non-conforming individuals were covered under Title VII of the Civil Rights Act related to employment nondiscrimination. This ruling is notable, too, because the decision was unanimous, and commissioners were appointed by both Republican and Democratic presidents. So, after this important decision, the message to our transgender friends is: please do not leave your gay, lesbian, and bisexual friends behind!

Hopefully, the EEOC will be able to expand its ruling to cover all LGBT people by considering also that gays, lesbians, and bisexuals are intrinsically gender non-conforming.

The protections in the United States against discrimination are extensive, as one would expect in an advanced democracy. They include:

- Employment
- Housing
- Credit
- Public accommodation
- Public facilities
- Federally funded programs and activities

A comprehensive bill to protect against discrimination due to sexual orientation was introduced by Bella Abzug in 1974 in the House of Representatives. Year after year it was getting more cosponsors, but it never got voted on. Fifteen years later, in 1989, it was reintroduced, focusing only on employment nondiscrimination covering sexual orientation under the strategy that a smaller legislation would have a higher chance to pass.

Despite this strategy of asking for less, almost forty years later, there is still no federal law against discrimination in employment due to sexual orientation.

Interestingly, most Americans believe that sexual orientation and gender identity and expression are already protected against discrimination in federal legislation and state laws. Here is the reality:

- There is no federal law protecting against discrimination based on sexual orientation or gender identity and expression.

- In twenty-nine states there is no protection against discrimination based on sexual orientation or gender identity or expression.

- In only fifteen states and the District of Columbia there is protection against discrimination based on sexual orientation and gender identity and expression.

- Six states provide limited protection.

As mentioned earlier, as of April 20, 2012, transgender and gender non-conforming individuals are the only LGBT people protected nationwide against employment discrimination thanks to an Equal Employment Opportunity Commission ruling.

There is still much work to be done to achieve the protection against discrimination in employment, housing, credit, public accommodation, public facilities, and federal funded programs that most Americans take for granted (and falsely believe is already available to lesbian, gay, bisexual, and transgender people).

Nondiscrimination is a critical battle for equality in our country because it affects so many people. Also, people cannot fight for other rights if they are concerned that they will be fired for being who they are. So the battle continues on this front, but we got a sliver of equality in one of the most revered institutions. Read on.

23.

Equality Goal: Marriage Equality

"Separate is never equal."

—The Dallas Principles,
Principle #3

The freedom to marry the person you love is the most prominent battle for equality in our country today. It has caught the imagination of a young generation, who cannot comprehend such discrimination. So, most people might expect this to be the longest chapter of the book.

It isn't.

That's because the argument couldn't be simpler: marriage equality represents the essence of who we are as a country. It represents freedom of religion. It demonstrates the key religious principle that it is not for me to judge others. It represents the pursuit of happiness. It represents the ideal that we live and let live. It represents that we encourage people taking care of each other in a lifelong commitment. It represents the idea that we do not want the government to dictate who we can marry. It is not about benefits and responsibilities; it is about showing your love and commitment to each other and the world with the word that everybody uses to express it: marriage. It is not about redefining marriage, it is expanding it by letting same-gender couples embrace the commitment that marriage means. It is about treating all couples equally. It is not about a separate, and unequal, institution such as civil unions, because separate is not equal.

There are five main arguments that are used to deny people the fundamental right to marry the person they love:

1. *"My religion says that marriage is between one man and one woman forever."*

This is a very valid argument. You have all the right to believe so. Nobody can force your religion to marry same-gender couples or to allow divorces.

At the same time, other religions believe that marriage is between two people who love each other—even if they are the same gender.

So how do we ensure your freedom of religion and at the same time allow others their freedom of religion?

It is quite simple: each religion can impose any constraints they want on whom to marry. We do not want the government to impose on you the wishes of another religion. So, the government issues *civil* marriage *licenses* according to its own criteria—one that treats all citizens the same regardless of their religion or their sexual orientation and gender identity and expression.

2. *"What about the sanctity of marriage?"*

Most religions consider marriage to be sacred. Naturally, only those couples who have married in that Church according to the Church teachings are bound by that sacred relationship. People married in a civil marriage, however, chose to be bound by civil laws and not by religious law in their marriage. Civil marriage and religious marriage are totally different.

3. *"For three thousand years, marriage has been between one man and one woman."*

This argument shows a complete ignorance of our history: several Native American tribes were polygamous; furthermore, the Mormon Church supported "plural marriages" (one man, several women) until 1890.

4. *"Why not confer the same obligations and benefits of marriage except for the word 'marriage'? Why not just have civil unions?"*

This was the position of President Obama until he concluded his personal evolution on May 9, 2012. Civil unions are a different institution, which is separate and discriminatory. It is a separate statute from marriage, and we have learned in our country that separate is not equal. In addition, it is discriminatory because it only applies to LGBT people.

5. *"Isn't marriage an issue for the states?"*

Marriage is indeed based on state law, but it is also a federal issue.

First, we need to repeal the Defense of Marriage Act, which prohibits the federal government from recognizing otherwise legal marriages of same-gender couples. Obviously, it is outrageous that the federal government won't recognize all the marriage licenses issued by a state.

Second, we need to ensure that a couple legally married is recognized anywhere in the country. Imagine that you are a heterosexual couple and that your marriage is not recognized in certain states. What would happen to your freedom to travel and relocate?

A well-respected Republican pollster, Jan van Lohuizen, found out that until 2009, support for marriage equality was increasing at a rate of 1 percent per year. Since then, it has been increasing at 5 percent per year across all age groups and party affiliations.

Many organizations are involved in achieving marriage equality, but Freedom To Marry (FreedomToMarry.org) focuses exclusively on achieving this equality goal.

We can have freedom of religion while letting all loving and committed couples take care of each other. Let's then discuss other equality goals.

24.

Equality Goal: Protecting Youth

One of our obligations in society is to protect our youth, especially in schools, in places of worship, and in homes.

We have to do much better.

What are the effects on LGBT youth when they become homeless because their parents throw them out of the house, while still underage, for being gay? What happens when schools are not allowed to teach about sexual orientation or cannot teach about protection to avoid pregnancy and sexually transmitted diseases? What happens when children, and especially LGBT children, are mistreated in the foster care system? What happens when LGBT youth hear the repeated anti-equality messages from so many elected officials? From their teachers? From their parents? What happens when heterosexual children are mistreated just because their parents are LGBT?

Are we a society who cares about our youth or not? Do we provide the safe space in which they can develop to their full potential? Studies show that 85 percent of LGBT students in middle and high school suffered from harassment in the prior school year (check GLSEN.org for their pioneering research). Harassment does not lend itself to a safe environment for youth to study, grow, and develop.

Too many young people have suffered due to some wrong-headed beliefs and actions from some elected public officials, some parents, some educators, some priests and church leaders, and other people who are supposed to help our youth. In 2010, all of this came to a head. In July that year, Justin Aaberg, a gay fifteen-year old, died by suicide in Minnesota. In September, it was Tyler Clementi, eighteen, a gay freshman at Rutgers University. Billy Lucas, fifteen and gay, from Indiana, also died by suicide. There was a national outrage, which resulted in a White House summit on bullying. An important resource to recommend to youth in distress is TheTrevorProject.org, which provides crisis intervention and suicide prevention services for LGBT youth.

More than twenty-five years ago, Harvey Milk, the openly gay member of the San Francisco Board of Supervisors who was killed in 1978 by another member of that board, put it best:

> And the young gay people in the Altoona, Pennsylvanias, and the Richmond, Minnesotas, who are coming out and hear Anita Bryant in television and her story. The only thing they have to look forward to is hope. And you have to give them hope. Hope for a better world, hope for a better tomorrow, hope for a better place to come to if the pressures at home are too great. Hope that all will be all right. Without hope, not only gays, but the blacks, the seniors, the handicapped, the us'es, the us'es will give up.

We have not solved the problem yet. LGBT youth continue to suffer tremendously. In September 2010, Dan Savage, a gay columnist, followed a few days later by Joel Burns, a city council member in Fort Worth, Texas, sent a message of hope to teenagers by stating that "It Gets Better." The video by Joel has been watched more than 2.8 million times, and the video from Dan and his husband, Terry, almost 1.9 million times.

As part of the ItGetsBetter.org project, many videos have been created and posted online. Here is a startling comparison about political leaders who made an It Gets Better video and whether their counterparts did or not:

- The president of the United States, Barack Obama, found the time to make a video for ItGetsBetter.org.

- The vice president of the United States, Joe Biden, did one, too.

- Republican contenders Mitt Romney and Paul Ryan did not.

- Former Democratic speaker Nancy Pelosi also made a video.

- Republican speaker John Boehner did not.

The list could go on and on. If we cannot take care of all of our children, what type of society are we?

Protecting our youth also means protecting the straight children of LGBT parents. COLAGE.org is an organization for young people with lesbian, gay, bisexual, or transgender parents.

The message to our youth is that *it gets better*. It is true that, after the teenage years, things change and do get better but not because the laws are equal. You can still be fired. You still cannot marry in most states. The federal government still does not recognize your marriage from one of the few states in which you can get married. And so on. It does get better because you can associate with people who respect you instead of immature middle and high school bullies. Still, however, you will face political bullies who do not respect the principle that we were all created equal and should be treated equally under the law.

The responsibility of the adults is to *make it better* for bullied youth. We need to pass anti-bullying legislation to end the torment of so many of our young people. We also need to show that we have created a society in which everybody is truly treated the same under the law.

It is time now to address the next equality goal also related to children.

25.

Equality Goal: Same-Gender Parenting

Many same-gender couples, like other couples, want to form their own families and have children. This is a fundamental human feeling and a basic right that brings stability to society. For the protection of children, it is very important to have legislation that treats all families equally under the law.

In October 2012, Sophia Bailey-Klugh, a ten-year-old, sent a letter to President Obama. It was unprompted by her parents. Here is the letter:

> Dear Barack Obama,
>
> It's Sophia Bailey Klugh your friend who invited you to dinner. You don't remember okay that's fine. But I just wanted to tell you that I am so glad you agree that two men can love each other because I have two dads and they love each other. But at school kids think that it's gross and weird but it really hurts my heart and feelings. So I come to you because you are my hero. If you were me and had two dads that love each other, and kids at school teased you about it, what would you do?
>
> Please respond!
>
> I just wanted to say you really inspire me. I hope you win on being the president. You would totally make the world better place.
>
> Your friend Sophia.

P.S. Please tell your daughters Hi for me!

On November 1, in the mist of his reelection campaign, the president responded:

> Thank you for writing me such a thoughtful letter about your family. Reading it made me proud to be your president and even more hopeful about the future of our nation.
>
> In America, no two families look the same. We celebrate this diversity. And we recognize that whether you have two dads or one mom what matters above all is the love we show one another. You are very fortunate to have two parents who care deeply for you. They are lucky to have such an exceptional daughter in you.
>
> Our differences unite us. You and I are blessed to live in a country where we are born equal no matter what we look like in the outside, where we grow up, or who our parents are. A good rule is to treat others the way you hope they will treat you. Remind your friends at school about this rule if they say something that hurts your feelings.
>
> Thanks again for taking the time to write me. I'm honored to have your support and inspired by your compassion. I'm sorry I couldn't make it to dinner, but I'll be sure to tell Sasha and Malia you say hello.
>
> Sincerely,
>
> Barack Obama

President Obama described what America is about. In the previous chapter where we talk about protecting youth, we are also talking about Sophia as the daughter of two gay parents.

Indeed, independent research clearly indicates that same-gender couples are as effective in parenting as different-gender couples. Here is what the American Academy of Pediatrics has to say about it:
(healthychildren.org/English/family-life/family-dynamics/types-of-families/pages/Gay-and-Lesbian-Parents.aspx)

Studies have shown that children with gay and/or lesbian parents are ultimately just as happy with themselves and their own gender as are their friends with heterosexual parents. Children whose parents are homosexual show no difference in their choice of friends, activities, or interests compared to children whose parents are heterosexual. As adults, their career choices and lifestyles are similar to those of children raised by heterosexual parents.

Research comparing children raised by homosexual parents to children raised by heterosexual parents has found no developmental differences in intelligence, psychological adjustment, social adjustment, or peer popularity between them. Children raised by homosexual parents can and do have fulfilling relationships with their friends as well as romantic relationships later on.

Here is the conclusion from a report of the American Academy of Pediatrics:
(neoreviews.aappublications.org/content/pediatrics/118/1/349.full)

There is ample evidence to show that children raised by same-gender parents fare as well as those raised by heterosexual parents. More than 25 years of research have documented that there is no relationship between parents' sexual orientation and any measure of a child's emotional, psychosocial, and behavioral adjustment. These data have demonstrated no risk to children as a result of growing up in a family with 1 or more gay parents. Conscientious and nurturing adults, whether they are men or women, heterosexual or homosexual, can be excellent parents. The rights, benefits, and protections of civil marriage can further strengthen these families.

Below is the conclusion from the American Psychological Association, in very clear terms:
(www.apa.org/helpcenter/sexual-orientation.aspx)

Social science has shown that the concerns often raised about children of lesbian and gay parents—concerns that are generally grounded in prejudice against and stereotypes about gay people—are unfounded. Overall, the research indicates that the children of lesbian and gay parents do not differ markedly from the children of heterosexual parents in their development, adjustment, or overall well-being.

Professor Judith Stacey of New York University summarizes it very well:
(en.wikipedia.org/wiki/LGBT_parenting)

Rarely is there as much consensus in any area of social science as in the case of gay parenting, which is why the American Academy of Pediatrics and all of the major professional organizations with expertise in child welfare have issued reports and resolutions in support of gay and lesbian parental rights.

The scientific evidence is clear. Despite this, in 2008, the state of Florida spent $120,000 of taxpayers' money for the testimony of Dr. George Alan Rekers, who was paid to testify in opposition to a lawsuit asking to allow single LGBT people to adopt in Florida—like they can do in *all* other states. Dr. Rekers, a professor and ordained Southern Baptist minister, has written extensively about homosexuality, parenting, and conversion therapy. He also testified on multiple occasions in the past against parenthood by LGBT people, as well as testifying that homosexuality is sinful.

Dr. Rekers was a major player in the past in denying LGBT people their equality. In the ultimate irony and hypocrisy, it was discovered that in May 2010 Dr. Rekers hired a male prostitute from RentBoy.com for a ten-day trip to London and Madrid, with detailed duties for his escort. These duties included sexual massages. Frank Rich wrote in the *New York Times* on May 15, 2010:

Thanks to Rekers's clownish public exposure, we now know that his professional judgments are windows into *his* cracked psyche, not gay people's. But there is nothing funny about the destruction his writings and public activities have sown. His fringe views have not remained on the fringe. His excursions into public policy have had real and damaging consequences on a large swath of Americans.

The suitability of an individual or a couple to be adoptive parents is always reviewed on a case-by-case basis. However, some states discriminate if the individual or couple is lesbian, gay, bisexual, or transgender, without giving them the opportunity to demonstrate that they can be good parents.

We need equal treatment under the law in the three types of adoption:

1. *Adoption by an individual who is single*

   Until 2010, Florida was the only state in which there was an explicit prohibition for LGBT people to adopt, whether single or in a relationship. An ACLU lawsuit resulted in a ruling on September 22, 2010, that such a ban was unconstitutional. On October 12, 2010, the Florida Department of Children and Families decided not to appeal the case. Finally, single LGBT people can now adopt legally in the state of Florida.

2. *Adoption by a same-gender couple*

   In ten states (California, Connecticut, District of Columbia, Illinois, Indiana, Maine, Massachusetts, New Jersey, New York, Oregon, and Vermont) and the District of Columbia, there is specific legislation allowing LGBT couples to adopt. In addition, in two states (Nevada and New Hampshire), same-sex couples have been able to adopt in some jurisdictions. On the other hand, Mississippi expressly forbids same-gender couples to adopt. Utah does not allow unmarried couples to adopt; since Utah does not recognize same-sex marriages from other states, same-gender couples cannot adopt there.

3. *Adoption by a member of a same-gender couple of the child of the other member (called second-parent adoption)*

   Four states authorize second-parent adoption in their

statutes (California, Colorado, Connecticut, and Vermont). In six states and the District of Columbia, appellate courts have determined that second-parent adoption is allowed for same-sex couples (Illinois, Indiana, Massachusetts, New York, New Jersey, Pennsylvania, and the District of Columbia). In one state, Utah, legislation expressly prohibits second-parent adoption. In three states, appellate courts have determined that second-parent adoption is not allowed for same-sex couples (Nebraska, Ohio, and Wisconsin). In the rest of the states, the law is not clear, and in some cases trial courts have allowed second-parent adoption. In Oklahoma, a ban on recognition of same-sex adoptions from other states was challenged and won in court in 2006 by Lambda Legal.

There is much work to be done in the states to achieve full equality in adoption by same-gender couples. All the major LGBT legal organizations have been involved and have been very successful with adoption cases. These organizations are:

- ACLU Lesbian and Gay Rights Project (ACLU.org/LGBT-rights)

- Gay and Lesbian Defenders & Advocates (GLAD.org)

- Lambda Legal (LambdaLegal.org)

- National Center for Lesbian Rights (NCLRights.org)

Along with the work in the states, we need to pass federal legislation. In particular, we need to pass the Every Child Deserves a Family Act, which does not allow discrimination based on sexual orientation, gender identity, or marital status of the prospective adoptive or foster parent or the sexual orientation or gender identity of the child involved. The standard, in every situation, should be based on the best interests of the child.

Given the scientific evidence and the absolute need for more adoptive and foster parents, it is horrible that some people are working so hard to deny these children an opportunity to live in a loving home. Our country is better than that.

26.

Equality Goal: Freedom of Gender

"Transgender discrimination is the civil rights issue
of our time."

—Vice President Joe Biden,
October 30, 2012

The majority of people understand the reality that sexual orientation is clearly part of a spectrum ranging from heterosexuality to homosexuality, with a middle ground of bisexuality.

However, most people see gender identity as binary: you are either male or female. The reality is that this is not what happens in nature. While the vast majority of us are either male or female, the Intersex Society of North America defines intersex as "a variety of conditions in which a person is born with a reproductive or sexual anatomy that doesn't seem to fit the typical definitions of female or male" and estimates that "the total of people whose bodies differ from standard male or female is one in 100 births." This is a complex medical issue that goes well beyond having a Y chromosome or not.

You may not have heard of the term "intersex" before and therefore wonder whether this is a new condition. Actually, a great sculpture can be found at the Louvre Museum that shows a beautiful naked female body lying on a marble mattress but with male genitalia. The sculpture is called the "Hermaphrodite Endormi" ("Sleeping Hermaphrodite"). It is about eighteen hundred years old.

So not everybody is clearly male or female from a physical perspective. Similarly, there are people who know that their true gender is not the gender of their birth. As an advanced society, with knowledge based on scientific analysis, we understand the need people have to live their true gender.

Transgender and intersex are different conditions, and organizations fighting for the rights of transgender people and intersex people try to keep them as separate issues. We respect this but note that both intersex and transgender people suffer tremendous discrimination and prejudices from people who are not familiar with the facts.

Similarly, some people are uncomfortable when people do not behave in the expected roles of male or female (this is called gender expression)—maybe a female who is "too butch" or a male who is "too effeminate" or a person dressed in a gender-ambivalent manner or a cross-dresser. Note that gender expression is different from sexual orientation. In any of the examples above, the person might be heterosexual, homosexual, or bisexual.

Many people feel more comfortable with a binary world ("black or white"), but this is not the real world or the world of nature.

Here are some of the hurdles and discriminatory treatment that people face about their gender identity or expression:

- Employment discrimination (fortunately since 2102, there are legal recourses)

- Lack of healthcare access and insurance coverage

- Inability to declare the appropriate gender in documents (passport, driver's license, Social Security database, and voting ID) to avoid confusion in real life

- Access to restrooms

- Air travel scrutiny

- Gender stereotyping

- Military medical and uniform regulations that discriminate against transgender service members

Some people have misgivings about allowing the freedom of gender. Some of these misgivings may be rooted in religious beliefs. Certainly people have the right to hold those beliefs. Other people have the religious belief that God created a complex natural environment.

There is a new generation of people who see gender identity and expression as a spectrum, not necessarily male or female. Like bisexual for sexual orientation, some people identify their sexual identity as bi-gender. This fluidity may be difficult to understand for the majority of people, who were born being comfortable with their biological gender.

A good representative of the new thinking is Stephen Ira. He is the twenty-one-year-old son of actor Warren Beatty and actress Annette Bening. He was born female and transitioned to male at age fourteen and concluded at age seventeen that he was gay. Stephen's video "WeHappyTrans" has received half a million views on YouTube. In this video, you can clearly see the looks and facial expressions of his father.

There are some notable organizations working on this goal of freedom of gender: the National Center for Transgender Equality (TransEquality.org), the TransgenderLawCenter.org, and the Woodhull Sexual Freedom Alliance (WoodhullAlliance.org), which takes the perspective of sexual freedom as a fundamental human right.

Most Americans share a common respect for our Constitution and the belief of not letting the government interfere in our most intimate decisions. Because of that, we need to ensure that people with a different gender identity or expression are treated equally under the law and can pursue their personal happiness free from discrimination.

Let's look into the next equality goal in the following chapter—a goal partially achieved.

27.

Equality Goal: Serving in the Military

Finally, on September 20, 2011, the repeal of "Don't Ask, Don't Tell" took effect. This was the legislation passed in 1993 that forced many service members, who are risking their lives for our freedom, to have to live a lie and not have the freedom to be themselves. The support for repeal had become just too big to ignore: 77 percent of Americans supporting repeal (*Washington Post/ABC News* poll, December 15, 2010).

The legislation to repeal "Don't Ask, Don't Tell" was passed in December 2010:

- The House of Representatives voted 250 to 175 for the repeal. Of those voting in favor, 94 percent were Democrats and 6 percent were Republicans. Of those voting against the repeal, 91 percent were Republicans and 9 percent Democrats.

- The Senate voted 65 to 33 for repeal. Of those voting in favor, 88 percent were Democrats or Independents, and 12 percent were Republicans. Of those voting against the repeal, 100 percent were Republican.

However, to gain some Republican support, the legislation was modified at the last moment to eliminate the clause that stated that service members cannot be discriminated against because of their sexual orientation. To be allowed to disclose your sexual orientation (which is the new policy) is very different from to ensure that are you are protected against discrimination.

While repealing "Don't Ask, Don't Tell" was momentous, we were let down by a Congress that did only half the job. It took more than seventeen years to get to this point. How many more years until we add sexual orientation to the nondiscrimination policies of the military?

Many organizations helped in the repeal of "Don't Ask, Don't Tell," but two of them played a key, long-term role: Servicemembers Legal Defense Network (SLDN.org) and Palm Center (PalmCenter.org). Both of them are likely to redefine their missions in the future. SLDN is already evolving, by merging at the end of 2012 with OutServe, a new organization created in October 2009.

In addition, several individuals led by Lt. Dan Choi and assisted by a new organization, GetEqual.org, added tremendous visibility to the fight not only with the public but also with elected officials, including President Obama and Senate Majority Leader Reid.

It is time to discuss the last equality goal—one that has been achieved at the federal level, but not in most states.

28.

Equality Goal: Hate-Crimes Legislation

This equality goal was achieved at the federal level on October 28, 2009, when President Obama signed into law the Matthew Shepard and James Byrd, Jr. Hate Crimes Prevention Act.

This federal law was named after two well-publicized hate-crime victims who suffered horrifying deaths. James Byrd, Jr., was a heterosexual African-American who was dragged from a pickup truck by three white supremacists in Texas. He was conscious through most of the ordeal, until his head and arm were severed when hitting a curb. The three supremacists continued to drive the truck, dragging the headless body for more than a mile. At that time, in 1998, Texas did not have a hate-crime statute (now it has one, but it does not cover gender identity or expression). The second person for whom the bill is named is Matthew Shepard, a gay student who, also in 1998, was beaten and left to die on a fence in Laramie, Wyoming. At the time, Wyoming did not have any hate-crime statutes either and still does not have one.

Although equality and protection of people would be expected to be a nonpartisan issue, the Matthew Shepard and James Byrd, Jr. Hate Crimes Prevention Act passed Congress in a very partisan manner, like the repeal of "Don't Ask, Don't Tell":

- In the House of Representatives, the vote was 249 in favor to 175 opposed. Of the votes in favor, 93 percent were cast by Democrats. Of the votes against the legislation, 90 percent were from Republicans.

- In the Senate, the vote was sixty-three to twenty-eight (with nine senators not voting). Of the sixty-three senators voting in favor, 92 percent were Democrats or Independents (Senators Lieberman and Sanders), while all the twenty-eight senators voting against it were Republicans.

The statistics above may appear partisan. The reality is that equality is still a partisan matter in the United States: the majority of Democratic legislators vote in favor of equality while the majority of Republican legislators vote against it. We see the same reality as we discuss other equality goals.

Equality should not be a partisan matter. Legislators of any party affiliation should agree to what most of the population already agrees with: every person should be treated equally under the law. A Hart Research poll in 2007 (two years before the legislation was approved) showed that 73 percent of Americans supported hate-crime legislation covering sexual orientation and gender identity and expression. More interestingly:

- Fifty-six percent of Republican men supported hate-crime legislation.

- Sixty-three percent of Evangelical Christians supported it, too.

The definition of sexual orientation covers not only homosexuality, but heterosexuality and bisexuality. So, it is a protection for every person (although note that some people identify as asexual).

While this equality goal has been achieved at the federal level, still much work remains to be done in the states.

There are many misunderstandings about hate-crime legislation:

CLAIM: If a crime is already penalized, there's no need to penalize more because the motivation was hate.

REALITY: Penalties imposed by the judicial system are usually based on motivation and intent. If someone kills somebody by accident, the penalty is less severe than if there was premeditation. Likewise, the penalty should be different when the motivation was hate.

CLAIM: Sexual orientation concerns a special group, and, therefore, sexual orientation does not need to be protected under the law.

REALITY: The law already protects other special groups subject to attack (for example, due to religious beliefs). The law needs to protect sexual-orientation and gender-identity victims because about the same number of them are attacked per year as are those attacked due to their religious beliefs. In addition, sexual orientation covers, by definition, heterosexuals, homosexuals, and bisexuals.

CLAIM: Sexual orientation is a choice (it is not innate), therefore it should not be protected.

REALITY: Science demonstrates that sexual orientation is innate. However, even if it were a choice, it should be protected since religious beliefs (which are clearly a choice) are protected.

CLAIM: Pastors may be tried under this legislation if, after their giving a sermon, a member of the congregation commits a hate crime motivated by the sermon.

REALITY: The hate-crime legislation explicitly includes First Amendment protections toward speech. Hate-crime legislation is about actions and bodily harm against somebody. Freedom of speech is always protected: we are always free to think and talk, even hateful speech. This legislation, among others, was supported by the Presbyterian and Episcopal Churches.

CLAIM: Federal hate-crime legislation means that the federal government will be interfering with local police.

REALITY: The hate-crime legislation has been endorsed by virtually all major law enforcement organizations (including the International Association of Chiefs of Police, the National District Attorneys Association, the National Sheriffs Association, the Police Executive Research Forum, etc.). The police force understands the hideousness of these crimes and wants to have sexual orientation and gender identity and expression in the federal hate-crime laws.

Why is investigating and penalizing hate crimes so important?

The FBI has a clear statement about hate crimes on its website:

> Investigating hate crime is the number one priority of our Civil Rights Program. Why? Not only because hate crime has a devastating impact on families and communities, but also because groups that preach hatred and intolerance plant the seeds of terrorism here in our country.

The most recent FBI statistics indicate that in 2011 there were 1,293 victims of hate crimes in the United States due to sexual orientation. This is about the same number of victims (1,231) due to religion. It is very important to cover in legislation both types of hate crimes.

Since 1968, there has been a federal hate-crime law that penalizes violent crimes against individuals due to their race, religion, and ethnic origin. It is well understood that there should be an additional penalty when somebody hurts somebody intentionally motivated by hate toward the victim's religion, race, or origin.

However, for forty-one years, there was no federal hate-crime legislation covering such obvious targets as gender and disability until Congress passed this important legislation.

Let's examine now how we keep score of the progress on all of these equality goals.

29.

Keeping Score

"Success is measured by the civil rights we all
achieve, not by words, access or money raised."

—The Dallas Principles,
Principle #7

It is critical to keep track of progress toward legal equality. To that effect, eQualityGiving (which I cofounded) pioneered two measurements: one at the federal level and one at the state level.

At the federal level, there are thirteen major areas of federal law in which LGBT people are not treated equally. These areas are addressed by the seven equality goals; some of these goals are counted separately since they may be considered by separate committees in Congress. Under this measurement, we have achieved:

- Hate-crime legislation passed at the federal level—full goal achieved

- Repeal of "Don't Ask, Don't Tell" has been achieved, but there is no protection against discrimination—so, partial goal achieved

- Nondiscrimination in employment has been achieved but only for transgender and gender non-conforming persons— partial goal achieved

So the rating is now two out of thirteen (counting partial goals as half a point) or 15 percent—we still have a long way to go to be 100 percent equal under federal law. The reality is that this is not rocket science. We know what needs to be done; it is all written in an omnibus bill prepared by attorney Karen Doering at the request of eQualityGiving (see next chapter).

Much more progress has been made at the state level—although only in a handful of states. For each state, we keep track of six of the seven equality goals (we do not track the goal to serve in the military since most states follow federal law for their national guard). Two states have reached a score of 100 percent legal equality for their LGBT residents. Can you guess which states they are?

If you thought Massachusetts, this was a good logical choice since it was the first state to offer marriage equality. However, it only scores 83 percent since it is missing a couple of important protections for transgender people.

The two states that have 100 percent equality for LGBT individuals are Connecticut and Vermont. Three states are very close: California, Iowa, and New Jersey—as is the District of Columbia.

Here is an example of why it is important to keep score with uniform measurements: one large state LGBT organization prepared its own study of progress in its state and concluded that the state was in the top five states for protecting LGBT individuals from discrimination. The reality is different: the eQualityGiving measure rates their state at 25 percent (which places it toward the bottom). One example of the discrepancy in the results is that the state organization gives itself credit for having a statewide statute protecting against bullying. That statute, however, does not list specific categories of protected youth. Research by GLSEN shows that without enumeration such legislation is not effective at all on protecting individuals.

Do you know where your state stands in LGBT equality?

Take the following quiz:

1. HATE CRIMES: Does your state have hate-crime laws that address violent crimes against individuals due to their sexual orientation *and* gender identity and expression?

   a) Yes
   b) Only sexual orientation is covered in state law
   c) No state law (only federal law)
   d) Don't know

2. NONDISCRIMINATION: Does your state have laws that forbid discrimination in employment for both private and public employers as well as in housing, finance, and public accommodations due to sexual orientation *and* gender identity and expression?

a) Yes
b) Mostly: sexual orientation and gender identity covered with the exception of public accommodation protection for gender identity
c) Only sexual orientation covered
d) No state law
e) Don't know

3. CIVIL MARRIAGE EQUALITY: Does your state have laws allowing same-gender couples to marry (i.e., get the same civil marriage license as different-gender couples)?

a) Yes
b) Civil unions only
c) Domestic partnerships only
d) No
e) Don't know

4. FREEDOM OF GENDER: Does your state allow a transgender person to obtain a new birth certificate indicating the correct gender?

a) Yes
b) Amended certificate (which shows the prior gender)
c) Decided by court order
d) Depends on city clerk
e) No
f) Don't know

5. PROTECTING YOUTH: Does your state have anti-bullying/ anti-harassment laws that specifically list sexual orientation *and* gender identity and expression?

a) Yes
b) Only sexual orientation listed
c) No
d) Don't know

6. SAME-GENDER PARENTING RIGHTS: Does your state allow all qualified LGBT individuals and same-gender couples to jointly adopt, as well as allowing second-parent adoption?

a) Yes
b) Only single LGBT people can adopt
c) Only single or joint adoption, but not second-parent adoption
d) It depends on the jurisdiction—some do allow it
e) Not tested—full extent of parental rights not known
f) No
g) Don't know

You can check the answers for any state and the District of Columbia here:
www.eQualityGiving.org/States-of-Equality-and-Gay-Rights-Scorecard.

As the federal and state measurements show, more progress has been made on LGBT legal equality in the states than in the federal government. In two states (Connecticut and Vermont), the answer to all the questions above is *yes*. However, in the other forty-eight states, LGBT people are not treated equally under the law.

Why are we shortchanging our beloved Constitution and not providing the equal protection under the law that it promises? The next chapter tackles this question.

30.

Equal Once and for All

"Equal laws protecting equal rights... the best
guarantee of loyalty and love of country."

—James Madison

In 2005, eQualityGiving created the equality goals. As we have
seen, this is the simple expression in plain English of what is
needed for LGBT people to be equal under the law. Interestingly
enough, the majority (if not all) of the LGBT organizations
structure their websites in terms of *issues* instead of *goals*. This
has an impact on focus, approach, measurements, and what
constitutes success. It has an impact on endorsements for elected
office as well as the expectations about what these candidates
should do once they are elected.

In late 2008, eQualityGiving engaged Karen Doering, a well-
respected attorney and expert on nondiscrimination legislation, to
review federal legislation and prepare a model omnibus legislation
to bring equality under the law to LGBT people. The result of her
work was the Equality and Religious Freedom Act. It covers
thirteen areas of federal law in which we are not yet treated
equally:

1. Employment in the private sector
2. Employment in the federal government
3. Housing
4. Public accommodation
5. Public facilities
6. Credit
7. Federally funded programs and activities
8. Education
9. Disability
10. Civil marriage
11. Hate crimes (signed into law on October 28, 2009)

12. Armed forces (The "Don't Ask, Don't Tell" Repeal Act was signed into law on December 22, 2010)
13. Immigration

Currently, for the thirteenth category we use adoption instead of immigration (which will be achieved once the Defense of Marriage Act is repealed).

You can download the proposed bill here:

www.eQualityGiving.org/Blueprint-for-LGBT-Equality.

Some people say it is not a good idea to introduce an omnibus bill in Congress since it would have to be divided into pieces and be submitted to and get approval from different subcommittees. This is true, but here are the important reasons to introduce an omnibus bill:

1. *Putting it in writing*

   Since we are seeking legal equality, it is obvious that we need to have a proposed bill with all our goals. This constitutes the gold standard of what is missing to be equal under the law.

2. *No more than others*

   The proposed bill demonstrates that LGBT people do not seek "special rights" as the bill basically adds the terms *sexual orientation* and *gender identity* to existing legislation.

3. *No less than others*

   This bill is also the standard to compare to partial legislation if approved in smaller pieces. How does a bill compare to the appropriate section of the omnibus bill? Are there any last-minute amendments that compromise our equality? This actually happened in the final negotiations to repeal "Don't Ask, Don't Tell"—important protections were cut at the last moment, as discussed in Chapter 27.

Once you understand the purpose of an omnibus bill, you will understand that cutting parts of it in the name of compromise means that *rights get denied.*

A month after eQualityGiving presented the omnibus bill in April 2009, a freshman member of the House of Representatives, Jared Polis (who is gay), said that he would be interested in sponsoring such a bill. Two years later, in 2011, he was seeking comments about what to include. As of March 2013, his proposed bill, which is just a compilation of existing bills, has not been introduced.

Some legislative efforts are difficult. For instance, creating a healthcare overhaul requires significant knowledge of how the industry operates, its effects on patients, and the various approaches to solving the problem. However, equal rights legislation is not difficult to conceive. What to include? Simply include everything in which LGBT people do not have the same rights as others. This is why it is called omnibus legislation. It should be the gold standard—not just a compilation of bills with their own compromises.

How do we raise awareness of the urgency for equality? Read on.

31.

What Happened in Dallas?

Two dozen activists, donors, strategists, and former executive directors got together in Dallas on the weekend of May 15–17, 2009, and drafted a unique document called "The Dallas Principles."

The essence of the Dallas Principles is simple:

Full LGBT Equality Now. No Delays. No Excuses.

This may appear like an obvious declaration. It was as obvious then as it is now, and it was as relevant then as it is today. However, in the last four years, we have heard plenty of excuses to delay equality.

Here is the background: just after President Obama was first elected in November 2008, as well as during the transition and early months of his presidency, there was interaction between his team and several LGBT organizations. The expectations were high. Everybody understood that there were important priorities to address first (the economy was in shambles, and his policy priority was healthcare). However, it was clear to some of us that many in the LGBT movement were too willing to wait for "the proper time" to achieve equality and that they were buying into the administration's approach to do it incrementally over many years.

eQualityGiving wanted to motivate everybody to push for equality right then, when the conditions were more favorable than they had been in decades, with pro-equality Democrats controlling the White House, the House, and the Senate.

In this spirit, we contacted several people to join us in Dallas. We were careful to select people who were not currently heads of organizations and were mindful of having a balanced representation of gender, sexual orientation, gender identity, and race, as well as different skills and backgrounds. They all accepted, but some had to cancel at the last moment.

Why Dallas? Because it allowed the participants, who came from all over the country, to meet midway (nobody except for the moderator was from Dallas). This would ensure that people wouldn't join just because it was convenient. They really needed to have the commitment to come. Why a couple of dozen people? We wanted to ensure that the meeting was manageable and would create an end product. Everyone had to have a chance to be heard and participate fully.

So, while eQualityGiving convened the Dallas meeting, the Dallas Principles were created as a joint effort of the two dozen authors, everybody participating and everybody sweating the details to have a great product.

What was the impact of the Dallas Principles?

First, it has become very clear that we were right to push for equality immediately. To the dismay of many LGBT organizations, equality did not flow at the speed that they expected in late 2008 and early 2009. We were making progress but not in the timeframe, in the quantity, or at the quality that was expected. Then, in 2010, the Democrats lost control of the House as well as many seats in the Senate, and progress come to a standstill (as the Dallas Principles group had predicted).

Second, because of the Dallas Principles, some in the movement adopted the slogan of "Full Equality Now. No Delays. No Excuses." For example, the Human Rights Campaign started a campaign (including T-shirts) with the slogan "No Excuses."

Third, the Dallas Principles became known well beyond the LGBT community. Vice President Biden was made aware of them, as were key White House staffers, key members of Congress, and members of the Democratic National Committee.

Fourth, the Florida LGBT Democratic Caucus adopted the Dallas Principles as its platform for 2012. After that, for the first time in US history, the platform of a major political party (the Democratic Party) treated LGBT people as fully equal citizens, including the freedom to marry. The Republican Party platform of 2012 is similar to the 2008 platform: an insult to LGBT Americans. Note that the Green Party adopted many years ago a fully pro-LGBT-equality platform.

Fifth, another positive impact of the Dallas Principles is that there is a growing conversation about *full equality NOW*. However, many still say, "I support full LGBT equality now—*but* now is not the time because we do not have a majority in the House," or any other reason. So, in reality, these people do not believe in full equality now; they believe in *equality later*.

As Dr. Martin Luther King, Jr., said: "A right delayed is a right denied." How quickly we forget.

So, take your sides: are you for *equality now* or *equality later*?

If you are for equality now, you can sign up as an endorser of the Dallas Principles at ActOnPrinciples.org/endorsers.

The text of the Dallas Principles and information on its authors is listed in Appendix 2.

Let's examine next what is needed to have an inclusive movement for equality.

32.

A Movement for All

"We will not leave any part of our community
behind."

—The Dallas Principles,
Principle #2

For a movement that asks for legal equality for everybody, it is important that we show diversity in all of our efforts. All heads of LGBT organizations believe in diversity. But much more needs to be done to really show that it is a diverse movement.

SEXUAL ORIENTATION DIVERSITY

Too many people are still mistrusting those who self-identify as bisexuals. They think that bisexuals are closeted gays or lesbians. Granted, bisexuals are a minority of the population, and, granted, when they are acting on their opposite gender attraction, they do not suffer the same discrimination as homosexual individuals. Bisexuals are still misunderstood and not represented appropriately in the LGBT movement (including boards of directors).

For the first time in American history, an openly bisexual person has been elected to Congress. In November 2012, Kyrsten Sinema was elected from Arizona.

Furthermore, beyond understanding bisexual people, there are many differences that need to be addressed between gays and lesbians in their approach to giving, politics, and social needs. In summary, many LGBT organizations will benefit from more diversity.

GENDER IDENTITY DIVERSITY

In 2007, the movement got a jolt when Representative Barney Frank said that he would strip transgender protections from his proposed Employment Nondiscrimination Act (ENDA) to enhance the chances of its quick passage—six years later, ENDA has not yet passed. At that time, many prominent LGBT people and the Human Rights Campaign sided with Barney Frank. They said, "Why not pass protections for gays, lesbians, and bisexuals now and come back later with additional legislation for transgender people?" Many others said, "We are all in this together. We cannot leave our transgender friends behind." In just a few weeks, more than three hundred LGBT organizations signed up to push for an inclusive ENDA. A year later, Barney Frank reintroduced an inclusive ENDA. Finally, six months later, the Human Rights Campaign supported it.

Since then, in April 2012, the bipartisan Equal Employment Opportunity Commission decided unanimously that transgender and gender non-conforming individuals are protected from employment discrimination by Title VII of the Civil Rights Act.

Most LGBT organizations include transgender people in their programs. However, transgender people are not adequately represented in the governance of organizations in the movement. As of February 2013, the following thirteen national LGBT organizations do not have a single transgender board member:

- Equality Forum

- Family Equality Council

- Freedom to Marry

- Gay and Lesbian Victory Fund

- Gay and Lesbian Leadership Institute

- GroundSpark

- Immigration Equality

- Log Cabin Republicans

- Movement Advancement Project

- National Center for Lesbian Rights

- National Stonewall Democrats

- Services and Advocacy for Gay, Lesbian, Bisexual and Transgender Elders (SAGE)

- The Trevor Project

Notably, the Human Rights Campaign, the largest LGBT organization, which has a forty-nine-member board, only has one transgender member.

Dr. Dana Beyer, an accomplished surgeon and transgender advocate, is leading a project of eQualityGiving to increase the number of transgender board members in the governing boards of organizations that represent LGBT people. An up-to-date list of transgender board members is available at: www.eQualityGiving.org/Transgender-Board-Members.

In the last few months of 2012, progress was made: Lambda Legal added a transgender board member, Dr. Jillian Weiss, as did OutServe-SLDN, which appointed a transgender executive director, Allyson Robinson, who also serves on the board.

While agreeing on the need for a larger number of transgender board members, executive directors and board chairs provide the following justifications for such a lack of representation:

- *It is difficult to find candidates:* This is true; this is why Dr. Beyer's eQualityGiving project includes a list (with bios) of seventeen qualified transgender people who are willing to serve on national boards.

- *It is even more difficult to find candidates who can meet the financial requirements*: This is true, as some of these organizations expect their board members to contribute or fundraise tens of thousands of dollars every year. However, organizations should remember that the primary function of a board is governance, not fundraising (as most like to think). Organizations can always have another board charged with fundraising or waive or reduce fundraising requirements for some board members.

- *They already cover transgender people in their programs:* This is true in most organizations, but it is not a substitute for organizations that claim to represent lesbian, gay, bisexual, and transgender people to have them on their governing boards.

RACIAL DIVERSITY

The importance of racial diversity (including on boards) is well understood among LGBT organizations. Progress is occurring, but it is still slow. The experiences and needs of white, African-American, Latino, Asian, or Native-American LGBT Americans are different.

POLITICAL DIVERSITY

About 75 percent of LGBT Americans vote for democrats. This is one of the most solid and consistent voting blocks for the Democratic Party. Yet this party did not bring to a vote the Employment Nondiscrimination Act in 2009–10 while the party had the majority in the House and Senate.

It is important to acknowledge that a minority of LGBT people are Republicans. It is critical to ensure that legislators understand that LGBT equality is a nonpartisan issue. The Log Cabin Republicans work with the minority of Republican legislators who support some LGBT rights. The majority of Republican legislators in Congress are strongly anti-equality. This is evidenced by their party platform, as well as by their votes against federal hate-crime legislation and repeal of "Don't Ask, Don't Tell."

ECONOMIC DIVERSITY

Much progress needs to occur in supporting the needs of LGBT people who are poor or destitute youth thrown out of the family's home or people with chronic diseases such as HIV who do not get appropriate medical care.

33·

Summary: Equal under the Law

A main foundation of American society is the belief that everybody should be treated equally under the law. This is same belief that is the essence of the gay agenda: to be treated equally under the law.

Here are the areas in which heterosexual, homosexual, bisexual, and transgender Americans are not yet treated the same under most states' laws and federal law:

- *Nondiscrimination in employment, housing, credit, public accommodation and facilities, and federally funded programs or activities:* Not treated equally at the federal level or in most states.

- *Marrying the person you love and having the freedom to live anywhere in the United States as a married couple:* Not achieved yet.

- *A safe environment for all youth to learn without bullying and harassment*: Not achieved at the federal level or in most states.

- *Being able to be a parent and raise a family like everybody else:* Need federal legislation and additional legislation in most states.

- *Free to match your biological gender to your true gender:* Partially achieved.

- *Serving in the military without lying about who you are:* Achieved; *not being discriminated against due to your sexual orientation and gender identity:* Not achieved yet.

- *Hate-crime legislation:* Covered at the federal level but not covered in most states.

What paths can we take to be better and treat everybody equally under the law? The next chapters show the different ways.

Part III:

Different Paths?

34.

Three Main Paths

There are three main paths to reach legal equality:

1. Courts
2. Legislatures
3. Popular vote

However, these same paths have been used to deny equality to people and even criminalize private, consenting behavior. One of the favorite techniques was through emotional, but false, appeals to "save the children." The courts would grant equality, as required by the Constitution, then opponents would label the judges as "activists" and seek to overturn their rulings by popular vote and even recall or impeach the judges.

In the past, in their disdain for some groups, such as African-Americans, opponents of equal rights went much further by going into a civil war and endangering the whole existence of our incipient nation. Many of these citizens who proclaimed to be for law and order would openly disregard court orders, such as for school integration. Or, worse yet, these citizens would take justice into their own hands, sometimes as part of supremacist organizations.

Fortunately, things are better now. We are not waging civil wars to settle our disagreements, but the willingness to keep rights and protections only for the majority continues.

As a country, we are better than that. In the next chapters, let's review how the courts, the legislatures, and popular vote can be used to bring equality under the law to *all* Americans.

35.

Path #1: The Courts

"Equal Justice Under Law"

—Inscription in façade of Supreme Court Building

In their brilliance, the Founding Fathers established a government system based on three *independent* branches. This independence among the branches is critical, especially for the legal rights of minorities. It is possible, but difficult, for minorities to get equal rights through legislation. This is because legislators, due to being elected by the majority, look first at legislation that affects the majority. They also may feel pressure from the majority to pass laws that marginalize unpopular minorities—such criminalizing what consenting adults do in the privacy of their bedrooms or legislating against interracial marriage.

This is why the role of the courts is to be independent and focus on the Constitution and equality for all instead of the wishes of the majority. One of the most important Supreme Court decisions for treating LGBT people equally was *Lawrence v. Texas*, which, in 2003, struck down all the sodomy laws (which also impacted heterosexuals). This was important because some people say that they do not oppose gays, just what they do in bed. Who are they to assume, much less judge, what consenting adults do in the privacy of their bedrooms?

Here is what the US Supreme Court had to say in its majority decision in *Lawrence v. Texas*:

> Liberty presumes an autonomy of self that includes freedom of thought, belief, expression, and certain intimate conduct.

> When sexuality finds overt expression in intimate conduct with another person, the conduct can be but one element in a personal bond that is more

enduring. The liberty protected by the Constitution allows homosexual persons the right to make this choice.

When homosexual conduct is made criminal by the law of the State, that declaration in and of itself is an invitation to subject *homosexual persons to discrimination both in the public and in the private spheres.*

In another important judicial decision, in 2004 the Massachusetts Supreme Judicial Court in *Goodridge v. Department of Public Health* acknowledged that there are different points of view regarding same-gender marriage:

Many people hold deep-seated religious, moral, and ethical convictions that marriage should be limited to the union of one man and one woman, and that homosexual conduct is immoral. Many hold equally strong religious, moral, and ethical convictions that same-sex couples are entitled to be married, and that homosexual persons should be treated no differently than their heterosexual neighbors.

In the end, it comes down to individual autonomy and equality under the law. The court continued:

Marriage is a vital social institution.

A person who enters into an intimate, exclusive union with another of the same sex is arbitrarily deprived of membership in one of our community's most rewarding and cherished institutions. That exclusion is incompatible with the constitutional principles of respect for individual autonomy and equality under law.

So the courts acknowledge that there are differences of opinion, but show that *the respect for individual autonomy and equality under the law should trump anything else.* That is the key principle that unites us as Americans. Still, some say the ruling is wrong, that they are "activist" judges creating laws instead of just interpreting them. The next chapter carefully examines this concern.

36.

Activist Judges

Some people complain about judicial activism, which popularly means that judges "legislate from the bench." These people believe that judges are taking the power from the people's representatives to create new laws and rights where none exist in the Constitution.

Some people would like the US Constitution to be read literally, as it was written more than two hundred years ago. The reality is that the world has changed in the last two centuries. For instance, the role of the president as commander-in-chief also applies to the air force, although planes are never mentioned in the Constitution. Also, fortunately, we no longer accept that any human being could be three-fifths of a person.

Most people complaining about activist judges are conservatives. This criticism is usually addressed from the right at judges who have supported the freedom of individuals to marry the person they love. The reality is that studies show that the US Supreme Court, headed by conservative John Roberts, has been the most "activist" in decades, including the controversial ruling in *Citizens United v. Federal Election Commission* (January 21, 2010), in which the Supreme Court ruled that Congress could not impose limits to financial contributions from corporations and unions. This was an expansion well beyond what the Constitution says (which is mute about the subject) and well beyond established precedents.

In fact, in *Citizens United*, the Supreme Court went well beyond the outcome for which the plaintiff was asking. This is extreme activism. Citizens United, represented by Ted Olson (who represented Bush in 2000 and won the presidency for him), only wanted a ruling that said that long movies showed on a pay-per-view channel did not constitute electioneering and should be allowed to be shown before an election. Olson specifically asked the court not to change precedent about campaign finance legislation. Breaking precedent, restraint, and moderation, the Supreme Court completely changed the financing of elections.

(Check the article "Money Unlimited" by Jeffrey Toobin in the *New Yorker*, May 21, 2012.)

Some politicians, such as Newt Gingrich, have gone as far as to state that the president should send the police to arrest a judge in order to compel appearance in front of a congressional committee to justify his or her rulings (on MSNBC's *Face the Nation*, December 18, 2011). Mr. Gingrich's demand is an attack on American democracy.

American democracy is based on three *independent* branches of government. The president (executive branch) cannot order anybody to appear in front of Congress (legislative branch). Similarly, Congress cannot compel judges (judicial branch) to reverse their rulings. Certainly, Congress can create new laws that, if they are constitutional, can have the effect of reversing a ruling. What a sad state of affairs it is when a politician makes such an outrageous statement and tries to undermine our democracy so heavily.

When we use the term *activist judges*, we are in reality attacking the independence of the three branches of government. As we said before, the brilliance of American democracy is the separation of powers. Legislators, elected by majority, tend to write legislation that represents the interests of the majority that elected them. Sometimes this legislation unnecessarily hurts a minority. This is why we need the judicial branch that, at the federal level, is not subject to elections to ensure that the rights of the minority are protected. We should all agree to support the *key constitutional principle of independence of judges*.

Fortunately, more legislators are seeing the fairness of creating legislation that treats everybody equally under the law, and they are supporting it. Read on for further discussion of the role of the legislatures for equality.

37.

Path #2: The Legislatures

"Religious beliefs are not a basis upon which to affirm or deny civil rights."

—The Dallas Principles,
Principle #4

In order to have legislation enacted that treats minorities equally under the law, we need to:

1. Support the election (and reelection) of legislators who are pro-equality. We need to support these candidates independently of their party affiliations (although most are Democrats) and their sexual orientation (many of our biggest supporters are heterosexual).

2. Follow up after the election to ensure that these legislators introduce and support pro-equality legislation.

3. Persuade other legislators to vote for equality legislation. The more they get to know gay, lesbian, bisexual, and transgender constituents, the more they understand their personal plight due to discrimination and the more they support pro-equality legislation.

The next four chapters present practical approaches regarding legislative activism.

38.

Endorsing Candidates for Elected Office

"Those who seek our support are expected to commit to these principles."

—The Dallas Principles,
Principle #8

Multiple organizations endorse candidates under different criteria. For example, the Victory Fund only endorses candidates who are lesbian, gay, bisexual, or transgender. This is a good long-term strategy. Clearly, having LGBT elected officials helps their colleagues understand the humanity of their votes and has been effective in passing equality legislation. However, there are heterosexual legislators who have been more supportive on equality issues than their LGBT counterparts.

Another organization, Log Cabin Republicans, supports only Republican candidates, but, contrary to the Victory Fund, they endorse independently of sexual orientation. Their pickings are slim. So, most times they endorse candidates who are partly pro-equality.

To reach equality under the law, we need to endorse and elect candidates who are fully pro-equality, independent of their party affiliation or sexual orientation or gender identity or expression. While party affiliation makes a difference in terms of which party has a majority, and therefore controls the legislative agenda, it is beneficial to have pro-equality legislators in each party. While it is good to have legislators who are LGBT, heterosexual legislators, being the majority, are vital to getting bills passed.

Volunteers and donors do not need to compromise anymore: *support with your money and time only those candidates who are publicly and fully pro-equality, including marriage equality.*

eQualityGiving, the organization that my partner and I founded in 2005, endorses candidates who support all the equality goals—regardless of party affiliation or sexual orientation or gender identity. Here is how candidates are categorized:

- *Pro-equality candidates.* They support *all* the equality goals. If they are in a competitive race (up to ten points difference from opponent), they are considered *endorsed candidates to fund.* If they are not in a competitive race (i.e., leading by more than ten points or lagging behind the competitor by more than ten points), they are considered *endorsed candidates.* You can give to them if you have a good reason, such as knowing them personally, but it is better to explain that you will support them when they are in a close race. In the meantime, it is more strategic for you to fund pro-equality candidates in competitive races.

- *Co-endorsed candidates.* This is the situation in which multiple candidates are pro-equality in the same race. You may choose to support one of the candidates for other reasons, such as party affiliation, sexual orientation, experience, gender, their position on other issues, etc. Otherwise it is best to reserve the money to support the winner in the general election or invest your money elsewhere if both candidates in the general are pro-equality.

- *Heartbreakers.* These are candidates who support most, but not all, equality goals or who claim that they cannot be public with their full support for equality. The strategy is to encourage them to become pro-equality and not fund them or volunteer for them until they do so. *We are past the point of supporting heartbreakers by donating or volunteering to them;* with so many pro-equality candidates to support, we need to focus only on those who have already evolved to being fully pro-equality.

- *Candidates to defeat.* These are candidates who are anti-equality because of their positions or actions (for example, by vetoing pro-equality legislation or supporting anti-equality constitutional amendments).

Most endorsement lists limit themselves to endorse or not endorse a candidate—missing the more detailed categories shown above.

For example, it is important to endorse, but not fund, somebody who is pro-equality and has a big lead in the polls. Similarly, a race might be a heartbreaker versus a candidate to defeat. While you may not want to support wholeheartedly a candidate who does not support us fully, you may want to work hard to defeat the opponent, especially if it is an anti-equality candidate. eQualityGiving's list of endorsed and co-endorsed candidates is available here: www.eQualityGiving.org/Endorsed-Candidates.

What if somebody asks you to support an incumbent member of Congress who is not listed by eQualityGiving as an endorsed candidate? With 535 members of Congress, it is possible that he or she was overlooked. More than likely, it is possible that the person is not fully pro-equality. There are two complementary ways to check:

- First, check whether they are cosponsoring all the major equality bills. The most effective way to check on this is going to ActOnPrinciples.org (which I also founded).

- Second, check their score on the Human Rights Campaign's scorecard (hrc.org). It indicates how they voted on issues. Although that scoring system has some flaws, in general you only want to support candidates with a 100-percent score.

An argument given for supporting candidates who may not be fully pro-equality is that it makes a difference which party has majorities in Congress and in State legislatures. This is a valid argument. While we may need bipartisan support to pass equality legislation, the reality is that the vast majority of Democratic elected officials support equality while the vast majority of Republican elected officials oppose it. Furthermore, Republicans are highly unlikely to bring pro-equality legislation for a vote (although a few of them would vote for it). So it may seem logical to give money to the Democratic Party to ensure that majority. In reality, it is best to support pro-equality candidates directly. You are in control. At the same time, it frees money from the party to support other candidates to reach the majority they desire.

You will also hear the argument in favor of giving money to a party to ensure a higher turnout of voters. You can do this if you wish but check other organizations beforehand that can be as or more effective at turning out the vote.

Another issue is whether to co-endorse candidates. If an organization has clear criteria for endorsement (such as support for all equality goals) then co-endorsements are necessary to provide the full picture to donors and volunteers. Take a poignant example: a race in which two candidates support our full legal equality. One of the candidates is LGBT. Which one do you support? If your endorsement criteria call for endorsing only LGBT candidates then it makes sense to endorse only the LGBT candidate. However, you need to disclose to the donors and volunteers that the opponent is also fully pro-equality. Some donors and volunteers will still pour their support behind the LGBT candidate, but other donors and volunteers may prefer to spend their efforts in another race in which their support can increase the total number of elected officials who support our equality.

Here is a list of the basic endorsement principles:

- *Support only candidates who are fully and publicly pro-equality,* as evidenced by the candidate signing a questionnaire. If they are not on the record (through a public questionnaire or public statements), don't support them (even if they tell you that they will support you once elected or that they understand our issues because they have an LGBT family member or friend).

- *Support candidates at all levels*—for president, for Congress, for statewide office, for State Assembly and Senate, for town council and mayors, for school boards (which are influential in determining what is taught in schools and anti-bullying policies), for police boards (to ensure that our community is treated equally), and for judges (very important endorsements, though often neglected).

- *Support candidates independently of sexual orientation.* In a race between two pro-equality candidates, it is best to invest in a different race (to increase the total number of pro-equality candidates). But everything being equal, it is usually good to invest in openly LGBT candidates.

- *Support candidates independently of party affiliation* (if you can accept their positions on other issues important to you). Even if you invest only in Republican candidates, invest only in those who are completely pro-equality (including marriage).

- *Do not support heartbreakers.* Instead, encourage them to become fully pro-equality (and then give them your support).

- *Support specific candidates instead of giving money to a party,* as discussed earlier.

- *Support organizations that are trying to ensure that our elections are verifiable and auditable.* This is critical.

- *Support pro-equality organizations that are trying to register people and get out the vote.* Ensure that these organizations fully support the issue of equality and periodically motivate their members to lobby Congress and state legislators for full equality.

If you decide to give to candidates based on a list from an endorsing organization, verify the following:

- What are the endorsing criteria?

- Are the endorsing criteria public?

- Do the criteria differentiate among candidates who are fully pro-equality and those who are not?

- Do the criteria require candidates to be public about their positions on LGBT equality?

- Do the criteria differentiate among candidates who need funding and those who don't (either because they are almost guaranteed to win or have only a slim chance to win)?

- Do the criteria allow for co-endorsements? This is critical information so that you can allocate your resources, if you choose, to another race.

A cautionary note: some endorsing organizations like to mention their win rates (i.e., proportion of endorsed candidates who won). The win rate is *not* really meaningful—any organization can reach a high win rate; it is a matter of how safe it wants to be in selecting the candidates.

As you can imagine, when founding eQualityGiving, we put much thought into the endorsement process. eQualityGiving fulfills all the criteria listed above. Its endorsements are nonpartisan and irrespective of sexual orientation and gender identity and expression (but both are disclosed). Currently, we endorse only federal (president, Congress) and statewide (governors, attorneys general) elections.

Besides eQualityGiving, other organizations also prepare endorsements. Most notable are:

- Gill Action (www.GillAction.org), which endorses mostly in state races. It is funded through the generosity of software entrepreneur and philanthropist Tim Gill. Mostly, they do not make their endorsement list public.

- Victory Fund (www.VictoryFund.org), which conducts campaign training besides endorsing LGBT candidates. They do not disclose their detailed endorsement criteria or whether there are other pro-equality candidates in the race.

- Human Rights Campaign (www.HRC.org). The endorsement criteria are not made public. HRC often endorses candidates with huge leads in the polls.

- Stonewall Democrats (www.StonewallDemocrats.org), which only endorses Democratic candidates.

- Log Cabin Republicans (www.LogCabin.org), which only endorses Republican candidates.

- LPAC (www.teamlpac.com), a new lesbian super PAC.

To achieve equality, we need to support pro-equality candidates—but all the money invested does not matter if the votes are not counted accurately. We are still not very good at counting votes, as the next chapter discusses.

39.

Counting the Votes

In November 2000, Americans learned a very important lesson about the most fundamental right in a democracy: the ability to accurately and verifiably determine who the people have voted to represent them.

The events of the November 2000 presidential election illustrated a series of problems:

- Unreliable machines that left punch cards with hanging chads

- Butterfly ballots that confused voters

- Bullies banging on the doors of the recount offices, intimidating and forcing to stop the recount

- The limitations of the electoral college as a way to choose a president

- The fact that the presidential election was not decided by 537 votes in Florida but by just one vote in the Supreme Court

The 2000 presidential election showed that each vote makes a difference. What has happened, then, in the last thirteen years to improve our elections?

In October 2002, by a bipartisan vote, Congress approved the Help America Vote Act (HAVA). This legislation has a very significant flaw: it funded the elimination of punch-card and lever machines while recommending that they be replaced by direct recording electronic (DRE) voting machines that cannot be audited. The good news is that there will be no more hanging chads; the bad news is that, wherever paperless DREs are used, there is no way now to verify the voter's intentions.

In early 2005, the Democratic National Committee established a commission (of which I was appointed a member) to analyze whether there was fraud in Ohio in the presidential election in November 2004. My research discovered the solution to one of the biggest problems in an election: how to audit the aggregation of the results from each voting station to form the final count for a district or a state. My solution got much attention and was codified into legislation introduced by Dr. Rush Holt, a physicist, who is a member of Congress representing the Princeton area and who is the foremost expert in Congress on election law.

Congressman Rush Holt has introduced multiple times a number of bills pertaining specifically to protecting the accuracy, integrity, and security of the vote count. His Voter Confidence and Increased Accessibility Act (introduced first in 2003) would have established requirements and provided funding for verifiable elections through the use of paper ballots and routine random audits, similar to his Emergency Assistance for Secure Elections Act (introduced in 2008). Two additional pieces of legislation, the Vote Tabulation Audit Act (introduced first in 2006) and the Poll Tape Transparency Act (introduced first in 2008), both based on my ideas, would have provided for a transparent and verifiable aggregation of vote tallies.

Although all of these pieces of legislation have been pending in several successive Congresses, only the Voter Confidence and Increased Accessibility Act and the Emergency Assistance for Secure Elections Act were ever reported by committee, and only the Emergency Assistance for Secure Elections Act ever received a floor vote. It did receive a majority of support, but it was brought to the floor under a procedural rule requiring a supermajority. The Bush Administration circulated a statement of policy against the legislation before the vote, and it failed to receive the supermajority required. Neither bill was again brought to the floor, even though various versions of each had earned a majority of cosponsors in the House. This has been a big misstep by the Democratic Party. Now is the time, in a non-election year, to fix this (as President Obama stated in his victory speech on November 7, 2012).

Meanwhile, the Republican Party has been very proactive and successful in passing legislation in several states to make it more difficult for individuals to register to vote and cast their vote. They claim that the purpose of the legislation is to ensure that only citizens vote—but this is a false argument since the number of non-citizens voting is extremely small or zero (for example, in a lawsuit in Pennsylvania, the state could not show a single case of non-citizens voting). The real aim of that legislation is to make it more difficult for certain groups of citizens to vote: seniors, minorities, poor people, and college students. These are groups that tend to vote Democrat.

This information is very relevant if you are involved in establishing equality through the legislature. You may support the proper candidates, but if we cannot verify that there were no errors in the vote count, and if we cannot ensure that all eligible voters will be able to register and vote without being blocked by disenfranchising barriers, all of our efforts may be for naught. So, if you are investing heavily in politics, either with your money or your time, you should consider supporting legislation at the state and federal levels to ensure the auditability and audit of elections and unobstructed voter registration and voting.

The best report on voting machine auditability and preparedness is *Counting Votes 2012: A State by State Look at Voting Technology Preparedness*, which is available for free downloading at www.countingvotes.org. The best reports on the recent changes to voter registration and voter identification laws are *Voting Law Changes in 2012*, *The Challenge of Obtaining Voter Identification*, and *State Restrictions on Voter Registration Drives*, which are available for free downloading at www.brennancenter.org.

Good organizations working on this include the following:

- Verified Voting (www.verifiedvoting.org)

- Brennan Center for Justice at New York University Law School (www.brennancenter.org)

- Common Cause Education Fund (www.commoncause.org)

- Advancement Project (www.advancementproject.org)

- Election Protection Coalition (www.866ourvote.org)

In 2000, counting the votes became all-important thanks to an activist Supreme Court, which decided the presidential election by one vote. After 2010, counting the money will be all-important thanks to an activist Supreme Court, which changed the role of money in elections by one vote. The next chapter further investigates money's role in elections.

40.

Counting the Money

Money has always played a role in politics. However, in 2010, the US Supreme Court elevated the role of money in politics to new heights when it ruled in a five to four decision that corporations and unions can spend unlimited amounts of money on political electioneering communications, including advocating for the election or defeat of candidates (*Citizens United v. Federal Election Commission*). The conservative majority of the Supreme Court also decided that such unlimited expenditures do not constitute "a risk of corruption or the appearance of corruption."

Who are they kidding?

Justice Stevens explained in his dissent:

> At bottom, the Court's opinion is thus a rejection of the common sense of the American people, who have recognized a need to prevent corporations from undermining self government since the founding, and who have fought against the distinctive corrupting potential of corporate electioneering since the days of Theodore Roosevelt.

This was a major activist decision, breaking precedent and not giving due deference to Congress (which had imposed limitations on such expenditures). This is exactly the opposite of the restraint that Chief Justice Roberts claimed during his confirmation hearings.

It gets worse: two months after that decision, the Federal Court of Appeals for the DC circuit ruled on the case of *Speechnow.org v. FEC*.

The result of both decisions is the creation a new entity: super PACs, which can raise *unlimited amounts of money* from corporations, unions, other groups, and individuals, and they do *not* need to disclose the identity of the donors. They have some trivial limitations: they cannot coordinate with a campaign and cannot make direct financial contributions to campaigns. But they can pay for their own advertisements, even targeting specific candidates.

This is not democracy for the people and by the people. Unfortunately, the only solution to this is an amendment to the Constitution, which is very difficult. One of the organizations working on this is FreeSpeechForPeople.org.

The next chapter focuses on passing legislation after elections.

41.

From Endorsements to Legislation: Act on Principles

Endorsing candidates who are pro-equality is critical for achieving equality under the law. Therefore, we have to ensure that they win despite unlimited and secret financing and although in most states there is no way to audit the results of the election, because of the use of electronic voting machines with no verifiable paper trails.

If, despite all of these obstacles, a pro-equality candidate wins, it is time to get into action—we need to ensure that pro-equality legislators introduce legislation that will bring full legal equality to all Americans. To do so, there is a powerful new internet tool: Act On Principles (www.ActOnPrinciples.org), which lists all the federal pro-equality legislation that has been introduced in Congress and identifies how each member of Congress is expected to vote on it. This tool also allows any interested party to update the vote count with any new information. Furthermore, web masters can insert in their sites a widget that keeps the up-to-the-minute vote count.

All parties in Congress and state legislatures use whip counts, which is asking the members of their party how they plan to vote on a piece of legislation. This helps the party leadership determine what to introduce for a vote. Lobbyists also keep their own private whip counts (covering both parties) to determine candidates who need to be persuaded. Whip counts have always been a very closely guarded secret. This new tool makes whip counts open and transparent—quite a revolution. Now there is a simple way to track legislation. This tool was created and is funded by this author; Donald Hitchcock maintains the website.

In the last few chapters, we have talked about achieving legal equality through legislation. What about losing rights by popular vote? Isn't voting the essence of democracy? The next chapter addresses these crucial questions and more.

42.

Path #3: Popular Vote

This is a democracy; let's all vote!

Certainly, voting is a critical part of a democracy. But should we vote on fundamental rights? How would you like it if people had a vote on whether *you* have the right to marry? Let's take the case that the person you love is from a different race. Should you have the right to marry? Should we take a vote on this?

In 1967, when the Supreme Court decided that interracial marriage should be legal, 72 percent of Americans were opposed to it (source: www.religioustolerance.org/hom_mar14.htm).

In November 2000, there was a vote in Alabama to eliminate from their statutes the prohibition against interracial marriage. Only 60 percent of voters in Alabama agreed to that removal, despite that the Supreme Court made it illegal to forbid interracial marriages for thirty-three years before that vote.

As recently as in March 2011, a poll of Republicans voters in Mississippi revealed that 46 percent of them believe that you should not have the right to marry somebody of a different race (source: www.religioustolerance.org/hom_mar14.htm).

So, was it an activist Supreme Court that allowed interracial marriages? In fact, the Constitution is silent about interracial marriages (as it is about same-gender marriage). Actually, when the Constitution was enacted, interracial marriage was forbidden in most states. Fortunately, the Supreme Court in 1967 saw their job as being *independent*. They understood that even if a very large majority of Americans were opposed to interracial marriage, they could not deny the fundamental right of a person to marry the person they love. Also fortunately, we did not take a vote in 1967 about whether interracial marriage should be legal. Clearly it would have lost. The lesson, of course, is that we *cannot put the rights of a minority to a majority vote.*

We have examined so far the three main paths to win (or lose) equality: the courts, the legislatures, and the popular vote. The next chapter will examine other strategies that apply to each of these three main paths.

43.

Winning Hearts and Minds

Whether you follow the path of the courts, the legislatures, or popular votes, a key component for each of them is to win the hearts and minds of the American people, the judges, and the elected officials.

Organizations like GLAAD (glaad.org) have worked very hard for decades to change hearts and minds through the media. Popular TV shows and movies have helped Americans understand better that there are lesbian, gay, bisexual, and transgender individuals in all occupations, and that, at the end of the day, we are all the same—we are all human beings with our accomplishments, strengths, weaknesses, and needs.

If you are an LGBT person in the closet, the most effective step that you can take to win hearts and minds is to come out to friends, family, coworkers, and everybody. Increasingly more people are accepting and embracing, but it really depends on many factors. Most of your friends and family may already suspect anyway.

If you cannot endure coming out of the closet or you believe that you are not gay or lesbian or bisexual despite having sex with somebody of the same gender, at least show respect for LGBT people by not tolerating homophobic jokes, by supporting equality policies in your workplace, and by voting for equality if you are an elected official.

You can express your support for equality in every day-to-day conversation—even with strangers. You can be an activist tourist and make clear to hotel managers, taxi drivers, shopkeepers, and others that you are LGBT and why you are visiting their town.

The most important minds to change are those of the people who can change the minds of many others. For instance, whenever you are in front of an elected official, you can always preface any conversation by saying something as short as, "Please pass LGBT equality legislation now," like a female service member who whispered to President Obama, "Please repeal 'Don't Ask, Don't Tell.'" This is what I did when invited to the White House in 2009. I told the president, the first lady, the vice president, the second lady, and my senator the importance of full LGBT equality. I also handed a letter to President Obama that said, in its entirety (with the italics and bold as in the original):

May 4, 2009

Dear President Obama,

Thank you for taking a moment to read this letter from a gay American.

I came to this country twenty-nine years ago with a Fulbright fellowship when America was the beacon of freedom. I got a doctorate from Stanford University, reached financial success, and retired at age forty. I became a citizen and lived the American dream.

But now America is no longer the leader in civil rights, as gay couples are not treated equally, like they are in many countries, including my former one, Spain.
Many American politicians are following your lead in a call for civil unions, a separate and unequal institution. You continue to express publicly your personal belief that marriage is between a man and a woman—which is clearly discriminatory and contrary to the practice of many religions, including your own.

When you say that you believe marriage is between a man and a woman, please know that those words feel like <u>a knife going through our hearts</u>. It is hurtful to us every time you say that, and it is harmful to our struggle for equal rights.

It would be helpful if you would instead say something like the following:

"As President, it is my duty to make sure all Americans are treated equally.

Our country is deeply divided on this issue.

*Some states allow same-gender marriage, some civil unions and domestic partnerships, and some states forbid it in their state constitutions. **The federal government needs to recognize and treat equally all marriage licenses issued by a state.***

*Marriage is also a religious institution. Since the US Constitution states that 'Congress shall make no law respecting an establishment of religion, or prohibiting the free exercise thereof,' **rest assured that the federal government will not interfere with religions' right to marry who they want. Some religions perform same-gender marriages, and other religions forbid it."***

I am available to discuss this matter with you or your aides at any time.

Sincerely,

Juan Ahonen-Jover, Ph.D.

Three years and four days after getting this letter, President Obama came out in favor of marriage equality. This letter is just one example of the combined effort of thousands of people who made it possible: we won the hearts and minds not only of the American people but of the president of the United States.

44.

Equal Rights and Businesses

"IF YOU DON'T LIKE GAY MARRIAGE,
DON'T GET GAY MARRIED."

—Billboard advertisement for Manhattan Mini
Storage

While awaiting federal and state legislation to provide nondiscrimination, we need to rely on policies adopted voluntarily by businesses. Since 2002, the Human Rights Campaign has kept a Corporate Equality Index; Appendix 3 lists companies with a rating of 100 percent. This index shows tremendous progress by American corporations: 110 of the top Fortune 500 corporations have a perfect rating of 100 percent (up from eighty-eight in 2012), and thirteen of the top twenty corporations in America reach the same perfect rating. Still, legislation to protect against nondiscrimination is badly needed since the Fortune 500 employs only a small part of the workforce in the United States.

Note that an executive order from the president requiring that all federal contractors do not discriminate in employment based on sexual orientation or gender identity or expression would immediately cover almost 20 percent of the working population in the United States. Such an executive order is ready for President Obama's signature. He indicated that he would not sign it until after the election. So, the time is now.

A good example of a company being pro-active about equality is Google, which, in 2012, launched a worldwide campaign called Legalize Love. It is about full LGBT equality, not just marriage. It focuses on countries with a homophobic culture and countries that punish being LGBT.

Another good example is Marriott, which recently joined a coalition to fight the Defense of Marriage Act. Marriott was founded by a Mormon, and his son, Bill Marriott, also a devout Mormon, is the executive chairman. While Bill Marriott personally believes that marriage is between one man and one woman, and he does not drink alcohol, he recently stated, "Our church is very much opposed to alcohol and we're probably one of the biggest sales engines of liquor in the United States. I don't drink. We serve a lot of liquor." He also stated, "We have all the American values: the values of hard work, the values of integrity, the values of fairness and respect." Indeed, these are the values of America and any good business.

A poignant video called *Find Your Understanding* was created by Expedia, the online travel company. It has been watched more than 2.4 million times. It is a wonderful example of a corporation understanding human nature. Watch it at www.youtube.com/watch?v=ThzdsnXeE28

A new issue has surfaced after the *Citizens United* decision by the Supreme Court in 2010: corporations can donate *unlimited* amounts of money for electioneering. And they can do so *anonymously*. For instance, a corporation may be giving to elect conservative candidates to lower corporate tax rates or reduce regulation of an industry. Given that most fiscally conservative candidates are nowadays also socially conservative, the corporations may be giving to candidates who legislate against equality. A corporation may even have a 100-percent rating in the Corporate Equality Index and may even donate to an LGBT nonprofit—while at the same time supporting candidates who are anti-equality.

To solve this problem requires external pressure as well as inside advocates (in which OutAndEqual.org and employee LGBT groups play a key role). This represents one of the most important and unresolved issues facing our relationship with corporations. It is also a difficult problem to resolve because corporate giving for electioneering can be impossible to track since it can be done anonymously.

In the 2012 elections, some corporations, supported by the *Citizens United* decision, took the unprecedented step of sending their employees "voting guides" or letters from the CEO asking all the employees to support certain candidates. For example, Wynn Resorts, which is the third-largest casino company in the country, sent such a voting guide to its twelve thousand employees asking them to vote for conservative candidates—many of whom are anti-equality. Note, ironically, that Wynn Resorts has a 100-percent rating in the Corporate Equality Index from the Human Rights Campaign.

45.

Building Coalitions

Not to state the obvious, but work to reach equality requires building coalitions. We need to:

- Work with the women's political community since it is a big supporter of the LGBT community. In the four states in which marriage equality was on the ballot in November 2012, women supported us more than men. In Maine, it was 61 percent of women in favor versus 47 percent of men. In Washington State, 57 percent of women were in favor versus 49 percent of men. In Maryland, the vote was 55 percent of women versus 48 percent of men. In Minnesota, the tally was 56 percent of women versus 46 percent of men. None of the four ballot initiatives would have passed if only men had voted.

- Demonstrate to the African-American community that the LGBT community truly understands its issues, its cultures, and its religious heritages, and that our organizations are truly diverse.

- Help the immigrant communities that, like LGBT people, want to be full US citizens and not second-class ones.

- Continue supporting the disability community, as they have supported the LGBT community.

- Ensure that governing boards for LGBT organizations include gay and lesbian and bisexual and transgender board members.

- Encourage Republican voters to support equality. In the ballot initiative for marriage in Maryland in November 2012, in many Republican precincts, marriage equality won a majority despite that President Obama did not carry the precinct.

- Show businesses that LGBT customers are big supporters of companies that support equality.

- Demonstrate every day to employers that LGBT employees perform excellently in their jobs.

The following chapter reviews what we've learned in Part III.

46.

Summary: The Paths to Equality

We have seen that there are three main paths to legal equality:

1. *Courts*
   This is the most cost-effective way. We discussed the real meaning of activist judges and why the current conservative Supreme Court is very much activist.

2. *Legislatures*
   It is key to have a high-quality and transparent process for endorsing candidates and then to follow up after the election to ensure that legislation is introduced, supported, and passed.

3. *Popular Vote*
   Putting the rights of a minority up to a vote of the majority is clearly the easiest way to lose equality instead of achieving it, but over time the majority will support marriage equality in some states.

In addition, for any of the main paths to equality, we need to continue winning hearts and minds and building coalitions.

We also discussed the newest issue in our relationship with businesses: some companies are very good with LGBT employees and customers while, at the same time, helping to elect anti-equality legislators who will have a detrimental impact on our rights.

We have examined formal paths to equality. In the next chapters, we'll explore what path *you* can take to make a difference.

Part IV:

What You Can Do In 2013

47.

It Will Happen Anyway

Some people are saying, "Gays and lesbians (and, to a certain extent, bisexual and transgender people) are now part of the popular culture. They have (mostly) won the culture wars. *So, why should I volunteer anymore or donate generously for achieving legal equality?* It is going to happen anyway!"

Clearly, LGBT people are winning the hearts and minds of Americans as well as people around the world. As this book points out, in the United States, LGBT people are still far from being treated equally under federal and state law. eQualityGiving's Federal Equality Index stands at 15 percent. At the state level, only two states (Connecticut and Vermont) provide full legal equality to their residents.

This is not the time to give up the fight, for three main reasons.

First, too many people are suffering and will continue to suffer until discriminatory laws are repealed and equality legislation is in place. They suffer because their relationships are not recognized. They suffer because they can be fired for being gay. They suffer bullying and much more. Their children suffer because their parents marriage is not recognized by the government. They are not asking anything that will cost the government money (studies show that allowing same-gender couples to marry saves the government money and enhances the local economy). They are not asking for legislation that is difficult to create: update the laws that mention race, gender, national origin, and religion by adding the words *sexual orientation and gender identity.*

Second, the four victories we had in 2012 by winning the popular vote in favor of marriage equality in four states did not happen by chance. The victories were won by carefully researching different types of messaging and going door to door to voters based on research on how to approach different people about this topic. These personal conversations were critical. Obviously, this was only possible through the generosity of so many donors and the work of so many volunteers.

Third, there are plenty of periods in history in which there has been a backlash against acceptance of minorities. It can happen very quickly. Many times you just need a charismatic leader or a popular TV personality to move the country *backward*.

This is not the time to give up. We are really close. It won't happen without our collective, intensive, and creative work.

48.

The Time Is Now

"Full civil rights for lesbian, gay, bisexual and
transgender individuals must be enacted now.
Delay and excuses are no longer acceptable."

—The Dallas Principles,
Principle #1

Undoubtedly, 2013 is going to be a historic year for equal rights in
the United States because the Supreme Court has decided to take
two marriage equality cases, besides a case of affirmative action in
higher education and a case regarding the Voting Rights Act.

For LGBT activists and donors, this is not the time to be timid. It is
the time to go all out and ask for full equality now. We have
tremendous momentum from the election and need to push
forward, especially during the first six months of 2013, when the
Supreme Court will be deliberating on marriage equality. The
Supreme Court may be hesitant to rule in favor of marriage
equality thinking that it is too soon. It is a time for extreme
creativity: multiple people and groups taking actions that will
highlight our humanity and need for equality in the eyes of people
and the Supreme Court. This is the time to show strength
simultaneously in the courts, with the popular vote, and in the
legislatures passing as many marriage and other equality bills as
possible. We also need the president to continue using his bully
pulpit, showing that he is a fierce advocate for equality.

One of the actions that should be taken is introduce all at once
legislation that will make LGBT people equal under the law. The
preferred method is by introduction of an omnibus bill, but if
members of Congress do not have the courage to do it, then at
least they should introduce bills covering all the inequalities; the
bills should be introduced all the same day to increase the impact.

Some pundits are reminding us that we do not have the votes, especially in the House of Representatives, and are recommending that, despite great victories for equality in 2012, we should focus on achieving majorities in 2014 (and 2016).

It is true that the Democrats do not have the supermajority in the Senate and majority in the House that they had in 2009–10. This was a rare event that last happened in 1978.

What can we expect in 2014? Predictions this early can be very unreliable (who could have predicted the ultraconservative statements by Senate candidates Todd Akin in Missouri and Richard Mourdock in Indiana, which gave two unexpected Senate seats to the Democrats?).

With the information available now, however, one should not expect the Democrats to gain more seats in the Senate in 2014. Actually, they could lose two or more seats. In the next election, the Republicans will have thirteen seats in play in the Senate—all but one (Maine) in red states. It is very likely that they will preserve all of these seats. On the other hand, the Democrats will have twenty seats in play, with at least six in red states (Alaska, Arkansas, Luisiana, North Carolina, South Dakota, and West Virginia). In particular, in South Dakota and West Virginia, the Republicans have announced strong candidates.

The House of Representatives was recently subject to redistricting in a way that favors Republicans in many states. As a result of it, in the 2012 election Republicans kept the majority in the House despite that they did not win the popular vote. So, it is likely that it will still remain under control of the Republicans in 2014, although they may lose a handful of seats. But Republicans may lose control of the House if their statements and policies continue to be detached from reality.

In summary, more than likely, the results of the 2014 election will represent no change in control in Congress. Possibly Democrats could lose a few seats in the Senate and maybe gain a handful of seats in the House.

Therefore, we should go all out now in 2013, on all fronts, in support of the Supreme Court cases. We need to act differently and more boldly, as addressed in the next chapter.

49.

Acting Differently

"Here's to the crazy ones, the misfits, the rebels, the troublemakers, the round pegs in the square holes... because the people who are crazy enough to think that they can change the world are the ones that do."

—Original text for the first "Think different" Apple commercial, 1997; narrated by Steve Jobs

An important way to accelerate reaching equality is by *acting differently*: pushing the envelope and creating new ideas and approaches because many times progress comes from unexpected sources. Below are some stories that highlight acting differently. Use them just as pointers. Having two cases in front of the Supreme Court decided by June 2013 requires all of us to take many, different, and creative actions to show our humanity and need for equality in front of the Supreme Court and the American people. We need street action (flash mobs, anyone? Sending pictures of same-gender couples to the Supreme Court?); we need legislative action in the states; we need the president to use his bully pulpit. Do not let anyone discourage you from taking action, because nobody really knows which actions will stick and resonate with the public. Go for it!

GOING TO THE SUPREME COURT

The legal organizations working for LGBT equality have done an outstanding job securing more and more victories in the courts, including the critical 2003 victory of *Lawrence v. Texas* in the Supreme Court, which decriminalized homosexuality.

Regarding the right to marry, the LGBT legal organizations have been building the case very carefully and wanted all their ducks in a row before going to the US Supreme Court. All of this changed in 2009 when Chad Griffin, a non-lawyer with significant contacts in Hollywood, asked himself, *Why not bring a marriage case to the Supreme Court now?* Of course, very aware of the risks, he then said, *What if we go to the Supreme Court with a dream team of lawyers?*

There are a couple of attorneys who come up when seeking representation in front of the Supreme Court: Ted Olson, a conservative, who represented George W. Bush in *Bush v. Gore*, the lawsuit in 2000 that decided the campaign for the most important job on the planet; and David Boies, a liberal with extensive Supreme Court experience, who represented Al Gore in the same case. What if you could have a conservative and a liberal, Olson and Boies, both on the same side in front of the Supreme Court, presenting the case for marriage equality? This would be a dream come true! Well, Chad Griffin made it happen (although his approach was considered controversial and risky by many heads of equality organizations). Chad founded the American Foundation for Equal Rights (afer.org) in 2009 and was very successful in raising the funds needed for this lawsuit.

So far, the Olson-Boies team has won, including on appeal. The case will be decided by the Supreme Court in June 2013, as well as a case regarding the constitutionality of Section 3 of the Defense of Marriage Act.

GOING BY FOOT

On June 9, 2012, activist Richard Noble completed the first solo walk for LGBT equality across the country, carrying the LGBT flag, and obtaining many proclamations along the way in support of the American Equality Bill—a single, comprehensive bill for LGBT legal equality.

Richard's 2,700-mile walk took fifteen months to complete. Even without receiving much support from most LGBT organizations, the walk achieved its goal of raising awareness for the need for legal equality and doing it now with a single bill.

GOING TO THE STREETS

November 4, 2008, was a sad day for equal rights: a referendum in California took away the right to marry in that state for same-gender couples. Eighteen thousand same-gender couples were married in the six months while it was legal. Fortunately, these marriages were not voided. This created three classes of citizens in California:

1. Those who could marry (and remarry) as they wish

2. Those who could not marry

3. Those who were married but could not remarry

Just two weeks after that vote, there were demonstrations all around the country in support of marriage equality. Who organized these demonstrations? The largest LGBT organizations? No. They were organized by just two people out of Seattle with a computer and much passion and creativity—an example of acting differently and boldly.

GOING WILD

A new organization, GetEqual, the brainchild of Paul Yandura and Jonathan Lewis, created quite a bit of good havoc by using civil disobedience techniques. Founded in 2010, it represents the spirit of the Dallas Principles:
Full Equality Now. No Delays. No Excuses.

GetEqual, with its direct actions, such as its members chaining themselves to the fence of the White House, is a key organization to raise awareness that we need equality now.

GOING TO THE WHITE HOUSE

President Obama had promised to repeal "Don't Ask, Don't Tell." Many actions helped to make it happen: the lawsuit won by Log Cabin Republicans, SLDN's lobbying Congress, donors' pushing key senators behind the scenes, a new organization (OutServe) of underground LGBT service members, and many other actions.

An action that was very different was Dan Choi and several others chaining themselves to the White House fence. It had a significant impact on the news and highlighted very publicly the need to repeal "Don't Ask, Don't Tell."

What should have been a small case of civil disobedience became a bigger issue as they got arrested and some of them faced trial (which they won after two years of legal battles).

GOING TO WORK

For thirty-nine years, we have tried to pass federal legislation to protect against employment discrimination. There have been no results as of yet. So Tico Almeida, an employment attorney who worked as lead counsel in the US House of Representatives on the proposal to ban workplace discrimination against LGBT people, decided to start Freedom to Work in the fall of 2011. This is a good example of an organization focusing on a single equality goal to get the job done.

GOING TO CHURCH

There are multiple organizations that take the soft approach to work with different religious faiths to make them more accepting of homosexuality. Taking a different approach, Mitchell Gold founded FaithInAmerica.org in December 2005 to directly confront the harm caused by religious bigotry. This is yet another example of a creative individual (he is the cofounder of Gold +Williams furniture design and manufacturing) acting differently. Mitchell Gold wrote an important book about LGBT, *Crisis: 40 Stories Revealing the Personal, Social, and Religious Pain and Trauma of Growing Up Gay in America.*

GOING TO GRADUATE SCHOOL

Chuck Williams noticed an important gap in our tools to achieve LGBT legal equality: the need for rigorous, independent research and scholarship on issues of LGBT law and public policy. So he started the Williams Institute (WilliamsInstitute.law.ucla.edu) in 2001 and hosted it at the UCLA School of Law to demonstrate the seriousness and quality of the research. The Williams Institute has done pioneering research on the census and LGBT demographics, economic impact of marriage equality, parenting, safe schools, and much more.

GOING AFTER THEM

There are several good examples of individuals going after closeted politicians who voted against equality.

For many years, through his BlogActive.com website, Mike Rogers reported about politicians that were in the closet while voting against equality. He was instrumental in having several of them to vote in favor of equality.

In 2006, Mark Foley resigned from Congress after Lane Hudson publicized his sexually explicit text messages and emails. This led to an outcry, and many observers credit this case with helping the Democrats to gain back the House of Representatives.

In 2009, Kirby Dick released *Outrage*, a documentary about politicians who are in the closet and vote against equality.

GOING YOUR WAY

The stories above illustrate the importance of creativity and acting differently.

Whether you are a volunteer, a donor, an activist, an ally, the head of an organization, or a bystander, by acting differently, you can achieve what old methods have not. Dream it... and take action.

50.

They Were Wrong

"Those who attempt to divide our community or to
delay and deny action on civil equality, waiting for
the right moment to arrive, will be held
accountable."

—Preamble to the Dallas Principles

Several well-known LGBT people in prominent positions called for
not taking risks before the 2012 election. The argument was that if
President Obama was to come out in favor of marriage equality or
even sign a nondiscrimination executive order, he could lose some
of the swing states and then lose the election.

By now we know that they were wrong. The president did come
out strongly in support of marriage equality, won nine of the ten
swing states, and won reelection. Furthermore, all four states that
had marriage equality ballot referenda voted in favor of marriage
equality, whereas the issue had lost relentlessly in the past without
the President's support.

Why is it important to highlight this? Not because those political
leaders are evil or ill-intentioned. On the contrary, most of them
are highly intelligent (some educated in some of the best
universities in the world) and well-meaning. They will tell you that
they spoke in their personal capacities. However, the press,
Congress, and the White House saw them as the leaders of the
LGBT movement (even if they may not consider themselves so).
What they were saying had impact. So, we need to highlight when
they were wrong.

One cannot lead from behind or continue with the same strategies
that did not work. The true leaders of the movement are those who
are in front, those who propose new ideas, those who think bigger.
The following chapters illustrate such a change in approaches.

51.

Insiders and Outsiders

For years, the politics of LGBT equality have been played as an insiders' and outsiders' game—the insiders being open LGBT elected officials, people with positions within the administration or the Democratic Party, or people in certain LGBT organizations (or those who wanted to be in those positions one day); outsiders were the rest of us.

When asked about LGBT equality, insiders would suggest for the most part, small, incremental advances and provide a rationale for why this was not the right time to move forward to fully reach equality. With the release of the Dallas Principles, which asks for full equality now, those insiders would say that they believed in equality, but that this was just not the right time.

The outsiders, in the meantime, would criticize the slow progress in achieving equality and would demand more advances right away.

The game would then be played in which astute insiders would point out to the demands of the outsiders and would make requests for more advances (while explaining that they understood the difficult position that the administration or Congress faced).

The first thing that some insiders would do would be to change the demands from the outsiders into requests—most insiders hate the word "demands." The second thing was to provide cover for the decisions made by the administration or Congress since LGBT "leaders" had been consulted. Of course, leadership is not measured by position but by vision and the capability to be in front of (not behind) the needs of those led and to possess the skills to get the job done.

The game needs to change now. It is time for insiders to be in unison with outsiders and demand to achieve full equality now. Without delays. Without excuses.

52.

Politics As the Art of the Possible

"Rethink Possible."

—AT&T marketing slogan

In the last few years, the buzzword sentence among politicians has been: "Politics is the art of the possible." It may sound like a reasonable approach, especially when you have Congress and the presidency divided among the two main political parties.

Thinking about what is possible is thinking in transactional terms in a world that needs transformational thinking.

The possible is the art of mediocrity, which is exactly the opposite of what America is all about. We are creators, innovators, frontier-seekers. President Kennedy did not ask, "Is it possible to put a man on the moon?" It was an impossible dream, but he led us to the moon. President Johnson did not ask, "Is it possible to pass the Civil Rights Act?" He did not have the votes, but he got the bill passed. President Lincoln did not ask, "Is it possible to pass the Thirteenth Amendment?" All his advisors told him it was not possible and the leaders of Congress told him that he did not have the votes. Lincoln did pass the Thirteenth Amendment regardless that the war was about to end (and, with it, his major leverage). More recently, in 2011, Governor Cuomo did not ask, "Is it possible to pass marriage equality with a state senate controlled by the Republican party?" He just did it.

As the AT&T slogan says, it is time to "Rethink Possible."

If anybody tells you that "politics is the art of the possible," suggest that we find true leaders.

53.

More Republicans Are In

"Let me take the pro-gay marriage people and the
religious people—I believe that there is a
connecting dot there that nobody is looking at, and
that's the Constitution. The question is not whether
gay people should be married or not. The question
is why is the government involved in our
marriage?"

—Glenn Beck, December 10, 2012

Certainly, it is welcome that Glenn Beck sees the connection
between our freedoms and the Constitution—which was the basis
of *The Gay Agenda 2012,* as well as this 2013 edition, which
presumably he has not read yet.

Like Glenn Beck, more and more conservatives are "in" and
understand that less government means that the government
should not interfere with the freedom of people to marry the
person they love, including same-gender partners. Increasing
number of Republican voters support LGBT equality. A few
influential Republican leaders support marriage equality:

- Dick Cheney, former vice president

- Rob Portman, US Senator representing Ohio

- Laura Bush, former first lady

- David Koch, a billionaire who, with his brother Charles, has
  given a record $400 million to Republican candidates in the
  2012 election cycle

- Paul Singer, a billionaire hedge fund manager who donated
  millions to pass marriage equality legislation in New York in

2010 and several other states in 2012

- Jon Huntsman, former Governor of Utah and Republican presidential candidate in 2012

- Gary Johnson, former governor of New Mexico, who was the 2012 presidential candidate from the Libertarian Party

- General Colin Powell, former secretary of state

- Ken Mehlman, former chairman of the National Republican Committee as well as the campaign manager for George W. Bush's reelection campaign

- Meg Whitman, former candidate for California governor, who opposed marriage equality during her candidacy

- Cindy McCain and Meghan McCain, wife and daughter of presidential candidate John McCain

- Christine Todd Whitman, former governor of New Jersey

- William Weld, former governor of Massachusetts

- Jane Swift, former governor of Massachusetts

- Carlos Gutierrez, secretary of commerce under George W. Bush

- Steve Schmidt, McCain's presidential campaign manager in 2008

- David Blankenhorn, founder and president of the Institute for American Values, who wrote *The Future of Marriage,* a 2007 book *opposing* gay marriage

- Newt Gingrich, while not coming out for same-gender marriage yet, was quoted by *The Huffington Post* on December 20, 2012, as saying: "[Gingrich] suggested that the party (and he himself) could accept a distinction between a 'marriage in a church from a legal document issued by the state'—the latter being acceptable."

Several of these individuals are not only expressing support or donating money, but are forming organizations or modifying the mission of their organizations to achieve LGBT legal equality.

We welcome these efforts, which will be very critical in 2013 and will help the Supreme Court's most conservative judges to understand the broad support for equality.

At the same time, we need to understand that several of these individuals have, at the same time, supported the campaigns of politicians who are committed anti-equality zealots. This conflict is less pronounced when these individuals spend their money in their own organizations, but when they fund a progressive organization, it needs to examine the bigger picture of accepting money from sources that also fund ways of damaging our rights.

The help we need from Republican leaders now is to change the minds of the leadership in the House of Representatives to allow a vote on LGBT issues and free their members to vote their consciences instead of a party line—not only for marriage equality but also for all the equality goals still pending. The rules in the House of Representatives are such that the consent of the House leadership is required to bring legislation to a vote, even if the majority of it supports it. At the same time, the Democrats need to ensure that all the members of their caucus support full equality now. The votes we are seeking from Congress are about each of the equality goals, not just marriage.

54.

Supreme Court Decisions

"The doctrine of 'separate but equal' has no place."

—*Brown v. Board of Education*, 1954

In a historic move, the US Supreme Court will take two cases in 2013 regarding the freedom to marry. Here is what is at stake:

MARRIAGE EQUALITY

The California Supreme Court ruled in favor of marriage equality in 2008. This allowed eighteen thousand same-gender couples to marry in that state during a six-month period until the voters passed Proposition 8, which declared that marriage was between one man and one woman only. The constitutionality of Proposition 8 and whether marriage is only between one man and one woman is now under consideration by the US Supreme Court (in the case of *Hollingsworth v. Perry*).

Hopefully, the Supreme Court will recognize the constitutional imperative, as well as the moral imperative, of treating every person equally regarding such a fundamental right as the right to marry the person you love. America was once a beacon of freedom and she would benefit from being it again.

Given statements by Justice Scalia, one can expect that he will work hard to confuse his colleagues with his personal and rather archaic views of morality instead of a reading of the Constitution calling for equality under the law.

The Court could deliver a range of rulings: (1) declaring marriage a constitutional right available to all couples in every state of the union, or (2) deciding that the eight states (soon to be nine) with civil unions or domestic partnerships should convert them to marriage, or (3) ruling that California should allow same-gender marriages, or (4) avoiding a decision based on the technical issue of who has the standing to bring this case to the Court (in which case California will have same-gender marriages again), or (5) determining that they should have not heard the case in any event (and therefore allowing California to conduct same-gender marriages again), or (6) upholding Proposition 8 and therefore denying more same-gender couples in California to get married until Proposition 8 is overturned by the voters. These are the six main options—there are, of course, a large number of variations based on these main outcomes.

Fighting this battle, we have a legal dream team, headed by Ted Olson and David Boies. These are the attorneys whom Bush and Gore selected, respectively, to represent them in front of the Supreme Court in 2000 for the job of President of the United States. Both attorneys have been very successful in portraying that marriage is a conservative institution. Certainly, Olson, who also served as solicitor general under George W. Bush, has the credibility in the Court to make such an assertion.

The organization leading this case in front of the Supreme Court is the American Foundation for Equal Rights, and they deserve our full support.

A consideration of marriage equality needs to bring to mind *Loving v. Virginia*, the landmark Supreme Court unanimous ruling that allowed interracial marriages across the United States in 1967. This is a ruling worth reading because of its clarity and brevity (less than five pages). It concludes:

> The Fourteenth Amendment requires that the freedom of choice to marry not be restricted by invidious racial discriminations. Under our Constitution, the freedom to marry, or not marry, a person of another race resides with the individual, and cannot be infringed by the State.

The concurring decision from Justice Stewart is even briefer and said in its entirety:

> I have previously expressed the belief that "it is simply not possible for a state law to be valid under our Constitution which makes the criminality of an act depend upon the race of the actor." McLaughlin

v. Florida, 379 U.S. 184, 198 (concurring opinion).
Because I adhere to that belief, I concur in the
judgment of the Court.

Let's hope that the Supreme Court has the clarity of mind to adopt a similar rationale for sexual orientation.

On the fortieth anniversary of *Loving v. Virginia,* Mildred Loving stated:

> I believe all Americans, no matter their race, no
> matter their sex, no matter their sexual orientation,
> should have that same freedom to marry.
> Government has no business imposing some
> people's religious beliefs over others. Especially if it
> denies people's civil rights.

FEDERAL RECOGNITION OF MARRIAGES

Although marriage for same-gender couples has been available for nine years in some states, the federal government still does not recognize those couples as married.

This clear discrimination was brought to light in the case of *United States v. Windsor.* This is a very poignant case: Edie Windsor and Thea Spyer got engaged in 1967 and were not able to marry until forty years later in Canada. They lived in New York, which, at the time, did not offer marriage licenses to same-gender couples but recognized marriages from elsewhere. When Thea died in 2009, the federal government imposed a $363,000-estate tax. If they were treated as a married couple by the IRS, the tax would have been zero.

Their case is now in front of the Supreme Court. It is difficult to believe that even conservative judges, while disagreeing with same-gender marriage, would not agree with the obvious requirement that the federal government, which does not issue marriage licenses, should accept a valid marriage license issued by a state.

This case would overturn Section 3 of the Defense of Marriage Act. It would not affect Section 2 of the act, which allows states not to accept the same-gender marriage from another state; obviously this is a nightmare for married couples who travel or relocate, and it should be corrected with legislation (the Respect of Marriage Act addresses such pervasive discrimination).

This case was brought up by the ACLU, and they deserve all of our support as they pursue this case in the Supreme Court.

ANOTHER OUTCOME: HEIGHTENED SCRUTINY

The Windsor case could produce another critical outcome beyond federal recognition of marriages: it could impose the *heightened scrutiny standard* for court decisions. Under this standard, the government would have to justify the reasons for any discrimination against LGBT people. This would immensely help achieve all the equality goals. This is yet another reason to support the ACLU in its lawsuit.

The outcome of the cases in front of the Supreme Court is likely to be positive for LGBT people, although the cases may be decided on technicalities, without creating significant precedents for future cases.

The next chapter discusses one of the most important outcomes that we could reach from the Supreme Court and what you can do about it.

55.

Loving Everywhere

Marriage equality is becoming increasingly prevalent with nine states and the District of Columbia now granting civil marriage licenses without gender discrimination. More states are likely to be added to the list in 2013 and 2014.

This piecemeal, state-by-state approach posses a practical problem: say that you are married and live in a state that allows same-gender marriages, what happens when you travel in or move to another state that does not recognize your marriage? Imagine the practical nightmare if states do not recognize your marriage!

This was the situation in 1967, when the majority of the country's population opposed interracial marriage. Some states did allow such marriages, some forbade it (and even in some states interracial couples legally married could be put in prison). The Supreme Court in the famous *Loving v. Virginia* case made interracial marriages valid in all states and territories in 1967. This was the most fair and practical solution to a patchwork of states with vastly different requirements for marriage.

Similarly, we need the Supreme Court to understand that same-gender couples must have their marriages recognized in all states and territories, as well as by the federal government. The Supreme Court can achieve this by requiring states to recognize out-of-state marriages or by requiring that all states allow same-gender marriages.

To show the dignity of our relationships and the importance that our marriages are valid everywhere, this author started a campaign called Loving Everywhere (LovingEverywhere.com). It is a call to action to send a picture of you as a couple to each member of the Supreme Court (whether you are a same-gender or different-gender couple) showing your humanity and dignity and the obvious need for Loving Everywhere.

56.

Make Me Do It

"I agree with you, I want to do it, now make me do
it."

—Franklin D. Roosevelt,
Comment to a group of reformers

Most elected officials want to do the right thing for their constituents. However, there are always conflicting interests, priorities, and urgent matters. In politics, the squeaky wheel gets the grease.

So even if an elected official believes in the cause of equality, we all need to push very hard to get legislation passed and executive orders signed. Telling them that we understand their other priorities and reasons does little to achieve equality.

The next few chapters detail the specific items that we need to *make them do it,* including President Obama, Congress, and the states.

57.

Make the President Do It

"Our journey is not complete until our gay brothers
and sisters are treated like anyone else under the
law."

—Barack Obama,
Second Inaugural Address

The president said, in 2008, that he would be a fierce advocate for
LGBT equality, and the quote above shows that he still believes it.
So, like in the famous quote from President Roosevelt, we have an
ally in President Obama, but we need to make him do it.

President Obama seems to be focusing his agenda for the second
term on three areas: gun control, immigration, and climate
change. Therefore, the LGBT community needs to bring equality
to the forefront. Undoubtedly the president wants to achieve big
goals. Let's make sure that *full* LGBT legal equality is one of his big
goals...and let's make sure that he does not do just half a job.

There are eleven main actions for equality that the president can
take on his own, without approval from Congress. The goal is that
he should do *everything* under his direct control for LGBT
equality—all in 2013.

1. NONDISCRIMINATION EXECUTIVE ORDER

The president needs to sign an executive order protecting federal
employees and contractors against discrimination based on sexual
orientation and gender identity and expression. Currently, there is
Executive Order 13087, signed by President Clinton in 1998, which
protects only federal employees (not federal contractors) and only
for sexual orientation (this does not include gender identity or
expression). There is also Executive Order 11246, signed by
President Johnson in 1965, which prohibits federal contractors

from discriminating based on race, color, religion, sex, or national origin.

As a presidential candidate in 2008, Barack Obama promised that he would sign such an executive order covering federal employees and contractors (a total of twenty-six million people or about 20 percent of the working population). This promise was not kept in the first term.

The president's spokesperson indicated in March 2012 that the president would not sign such an order until later (implying after the 2012 election). There is no justification for any more waiting since such an executive order has been drafted and vetted, and it has been ready for President Obama's signature for more than a year.

A poll by the Center for American Progress showed in April 2011 that 69 percent of likely voters in 2012 would support President Obama issuing such an executive order (this includes 83 percent of Democrats, 69 percent of Independents, and 53 percent of Republicans). So, no more delays.

This executive order is important because then the performance of the contractors regarding nondiscrimination for sexual orientation and gender identity and expression would be part of the regular reviews performed by the Labor Department's Office of Federal Contract Compliance Programs. So, the department could initiate investigations based on employees' complaints or third-party complaints and even on its own since, many times, employees are reluctant to file a formal complaint. Furthermore, the department could conduct nondiscrimination trainings at the beginning of a federal contract. This is why this executive order is so important in addition to state and federal legislation.

2. MARRIAGE EQUALITY

President Obama took an important step in early 2013 in support of marriage equality: he asked the Department of Justice to file briefs with the Supreme Court regarding the two cases that it is reviewing this year. The brief supporting marriage equality, however, is limited to eight states (soon to be nine states) that have civil unions or domestic partnerships. The Department of Justice should have made the case for marriage equality in all states and territories. Imagine the nightmare that despite being legally married when you travel or relocate to another state you are not considered married. We need a Supreme Court decision similar to *Loving v. Virginia*. We need to speed up equality—too many people are suffering every day that we delay.

3. OTHER POLICIES

A group of LGBT organizations prepared, documented, and published on the web a list of eighty-two federal policy changes listed by agency. They delivered it to the Obama transition team in December 2008. Their most recent update on the web lists sixteen policy changes. This is significant but leaves 80 percent of the changes still pending.

Why not insist on a presidential executive order that requires all the government offices under his control to ensure full equal treatment independent of sexual orientation and gender identity within six months? It could provide as minimum requirements the rest of the eighty-two changes pending. It should require a report within six months of the changes made, as well as an ombudsman for equality for each agency (if none exists).

4. DON'T ASK DON'T TELL

Here are the main items left to accomplish:

1. Revise the Department of Defense Equal Opportunity Policy to add sexual orientation and gender identity.

2. Amend military medical and uniform regulations that discriminate against transgender service members.

3. Treat all married service members equally. There are still significant differences in treatment based on same-gender or different-gender marriages. While this is mostly due to the Defense of Marriage Act, the reality is that the Department of Defense has leeway that other departments do not.

The new secretary of defense should ensure that these items get done without delay.

5. IMMIGRATION REFORM

The president should approve a policy change to keep married bi-national couples in the country while the Supreme Court decides on the constitutionality of the Defense of Marriage Act and until Congress passes comprehensive immigration reform. He should also revisit the administrative policies to grant asylum to LGBT people from other countries who need it so much. This would be in line with the administrative actions that he took for young undocumented immigrants, popularly known as the Dreamers.

6. TRANSGENDER MEDICAL CARE

The president should also expand the medical care available under Medicare and Medicaid for transgender people.

7. CABINET MEMBERS

President Obama should appoint an *openly* LGBT cabinet member. This would be an important first in history. Among the qualified people are Fred Hochberg, currently the president of the Export-Import Bank and previously the head of the Small Business Administration, and John Berry, who heads the Office of Personnel Management.

Incidentally, another important equality signal that the president could send is to fill half of his cabinet appointments with women and half with men. Clearly, there are women who are imminently qualified for any cabinet position. This was done in Spain by President Zapatero nine years ago.

8. JUDICIAL APPOINTMENTS

Clearly, President Obama should appoint more LGBT people to the federal bench and even the Supreme Court (one of the leading candidates is Kathleen Sullivan, former professor of constitutional law at Harvard and former dean of Stanford Law School).

9. OTHER APPOINTMENTS

A key position that the president needs to fill without more delays is the fifth commissioner to the Equal Employment Opportunity Commission, which ruled in 2012 that transgender people are protected against employment discrimination under Title VII of the Civil Rights Act.

10. ORGANIZING FOR ACTION

The president has indicated that he will use his campaign group, Organizing for Action (formerly Organizing for America), and its mailing list to rally Americans in grassroots efforts to pass his legislative agenda.

He should use this list to pass legislation for LGBT equality. After all, lesbian, gay, bisexual, and transgender people were significant contributors to and volunteers for his campaign.

11. FIERCE ADVOCATE

President Obama promised five years ago to be a fierce advocate for the LGBT community. He now has the opportunity to act on it. It is imperative to show to the Supreme Court momentum on equality in anticipation of their decisions on the two marriage cases in June 2013. President Obama can contribute to that momentum by taking all the executive actions outlined in this chapter, which do not require approval from Congress.

An important step President Obama took was to use the 2013 State of the Union speech to outline that equality under the law is one of the key themes that unite all of us as Americans. This is an important moral message to the American people, Congress, and the Supreme Court.

58.

Make Congress Do It

"The establishment and guardianship of full civil
rights is a non-partisan issue."

—The Dallas Principles,
Principle #5

For too many years, the strategy to pass equality legislation in
Congress has been twofold: first, make compromises and dilute
the legislation (making it less equal) to gain more votes. Second,
do not bring the legislation for a vote until we had enough votes to
pass it. This is the strategy followed since 1974, when a
comprehensive nondiscrimination legislation was introduced by
Congresswoman Bella Abzug and later limited by others to
employment only. Despite employment nondiscrimination
legislation being supported by a majority of American voters,
including a majority of Republican voters, Congress has not yet
voted on it.

That strategy was driven by the fear that if a bill was taken for a
vote and failed, it would be difficult to erase in the minds of
legislators and the public.

Let's erase the fear and turn the tables: let's take the vote and see
who does not support equality legislation, and let the constituents
know.

Clearly, the House of Representatives, which is controlled by the
Republicans, is unlikely to initiate equality legislation. The
strategy should be to initiate such legislation in the Senate and put
it for a vote, even if it filibustered by the Republicans. Let them be
on record. Then push it in the House as an amendment to a must-
pass bill and expect that some prominent Republicans (like those
listed in Chapter 53) assist, along with organizations such as the
Log Cabin Republicans. The expectation would be that the House
Republican leadership would free its party members to vote their
consciences.

Another possibility would be for 218 members of Congress to sign a discharge petition to request that a bill is voted. However, the rules in the House allow the speaker of the House to ignore such a petition. Therefore, still it is critical for influential Republicans to directly lobby Speaker Boehner. It's time to think bigger and act differently.

Below is the key legislation that needs to be passed by Congress for each equality goal.

EQUALITY GOAL: NONDISCRIMINATION

We need to pass federal nondiscrimination legislation that covers sexual orientation and gender identity and expression. Given how committees in Congress work, it might be necessary to have separate legislation covering, respectively, employment, housing, credit, public accommodation, public facilities, and federally funded programs and activities.

The main question is: do we proceed by amending the Civil Rights Act (CRA) to include sexual orientation and gender identity and expression or we create separate bills from the CRA (the current approach)? Some people believe that the Civil Rights Act should not be expanded to cover other groups or that opening it for debate may bring undesirable changes to the current CRA. The reality is that Title VII has been expanded in the past. President Obama could simply state that he would support an expansion of the Civil Rights Act to add sexual orientation and gender identity and expression but would veto any other modifications that would limit existing rights to any other group. The president, so far, is not providing such important leadership. Nondiscrimination legislation is supported by a majority of Republican voters and an even larger majority of Democratic voters.

If Congress pursues the route of separate bills, we need to watch that any exemptions given to religious organizations and corporations are the same as the ones given in the Civil Rights Act. Exemptions are usually added to bills at the last minute, often for the worse. There is a possibility that, with a separate bill, we could get some clauses that are more advantageous to the LGBT community than what would be available with the Civil Rights Act, but this is not the gay agenda: we want legal equality—the same rights as other groups. So the most coherent solution is to add the words "sexual orientation and gender identity" to existing nondiscrimination federal legislation.

In October 2007, Representative Barney Frank, who was the senior LGBT member in Congress, decided to strip gender identity and expression protections from the Employment Nondiscrimination Act that he was proposing for a vote. This was a wake-up call for the movement for LGBT equality. In a matter of days, more than three hundred organizations signed up opposing such a move. The National Center for Transgender Equality (TransEquality.org) and the National Gay and Lesbian Task Force (TheTaskForce.org) took the lead. In the meantime, it took the Human Rights Campaign (HRC.org), the largest LGBT organization, eighteen months to come on board.

In the fall of 2011, Freedom To Work (FreedomToWork.org) was founded. It focuses on passing employment nondiscrimination legislation, and it has already brought significant experience to this fight. From the corporate side, OutAndEqual.org is dedicated to creating safe and equitable workplaces for LGBT employees.

Another approach to nondiscrimination can be to consider that sexual orientation is nothing more than a variant form of gender expression, therefore discrimination against people based on their sexual orientation is simply a subset of sex discrimination. Such reasoning was used over the past few years to provide trans and gender non-conforming persons both constitutional as well as federal employment protections under Title VII of the 1964 Civil Rights Act.

EQUALITY GOAL: MARRIAGE EQUALITY

The type of marriage equality legislation needed to be introduced in Congress depends heavily on the results of the cases pending currently in front of the Supreme Court, as described in detail in Chapter 54.

It is reasonable to expect that the Supreme Court will rule that the federal government needs to recognize marriages legally entered in a state. The issue to watch is whether it will limit the recognition of a marriage to married couples living in a state in which same-gender marriage is legal. This would limit the freedom of same-gender couples to travel and relocate (or face losing recognition of their marriages by the federal government). In this case, it would be imperative to pass the Respect for Marriage Act. This legislation is supported by President Obama, and it is very concise (three paragraphs). It simply states that the federal government will recognize any marriage that was legal in the state or jurisdiction in which it was entered, independent of where the couple lives. When first introduced in 2009, the Respect for Marriage Act had 120 cosponsors. At the end of 2012, it had 159 cosponsors, including several Republicans. It is still shy of the 218 majority, but this is a record number. If the Republican leadership allows for a vote and allows its members to vote their consciences, it is very likely to pass in the House and similarly in the Senate. This legislation would also apply to different-gender couples, the federal government only recognizes the marriage if it is recognized in the state where the couple lives. For most heterosexual couples this is not an issue (if becomes an issue if you married say at age 16 and your new state recognizes only marriages after age 18).

Meanwhile, bi-national same-gender couples should be part of the Comprehensive Immigration Reform, as well as LGBT asylum-seekers.

EQUALITY GOAL: PROTECTING YOUTH

Our obligation to LGBT children is to *make it better*. Here is what urgently needs to be done:

1. Pass federal legislation forbidding bullying and harassment in schools for *all* youth. Studies show that this type of legislation is not only critical for the physical and mental welfare of all students but also decreases school absence by bullied students. This legislation should specifically list sexual orientation and gender identity and expression. Research by GLSEN shows that statutes that do not specifically enumerate sexual orientation and gender identity provide no more benefit to students than not having any law at all.

2. Advocate strongly for reproductive, sexual, and mental health education that is responsible and age-appropriate. Abstinence-until marriage programs have been proven not to work—even less with lesbian, gay, bisexual, and transgender youth, who are not allowed in most states to

marry the person they love. AdvocatesForYouth.org is a good organization pursuing this goal.

EQUALITY GOAL: PARENTING

Ensure that children can be placed in families for adoption or foster care without discrimination based on the sexual orientation or gender identity or expression of the parents or the child. Also, the marital status of the parent(s) must not be a consideration. This is part of the Every Child Deserves a Family Bill introduced in the last Congress (but not voted through by either house).

EQUALITY GOAL: FREEDOM OF GENDER

The goals here are:

1. Amend the Americans with Disability Act (ADA) to cover transsexualism.

2. Pass the Violence against Women Act (including LGBT). This was accomplished as this book went to press.

EQUALITY GOAL: SERVING IN THE MILITARY

Here is what is left to accomplish:

1. Enact legislation that specifically protects against discrimination based on sexual orientation and gender identity in the military.

2. De-penalize sodomy, as ruled by the US Supreme Court in *Lawrence v. Texas*, by revoking Article 125 of the Uniform Code of Military Justice (UCMJ). Article 125 forbids sodomy, whether among people of the same-gender or different gender. Congress needs to revoke Article 125, as the military has been requesting for years, since it is clearly understood that what consenting adults do in private is exactly that: private.

3. To fully achieve equality in the military will require Congress to act again; otherwise, a future administration could ban

LGBT members from serving by using a directive from the Department of Defense—without need for an act of Congress or an executive order from the president.

For an up-to-date analysis of what still needs to be done, you can check the list maintained by Ret. Captain Tom Carpenter, Esq., at www.eQualityGiving.org/DADT.

If Congress doesn't act, another venue is the lawsuit that the Log Cabin Republicans are pursuing with the intention of proving to the Supreme Court, if necessary, that discrimination of LGBT people in the military is unconstitutional.

59.

Reaching 100 Percent in the States

We can divide the states into three groups.

The first is the two states (Connecticut and Vermont) that provide full equality to their LGBT residents according to eQualityGiving's scorecard.

The second group is the eighteen states and the District of Columbia that, with a laser focus on full equality, could reach it in 2013 and join the first group.

The third consists of the thirty other states lagging significantly behind on equality.

This chapter addresses the second group, and the next chapter discusses the third group.

This is the time for a big push in the states that could get to 100-percent equality this year. The question to ask each state is: what statutes are missing for equal treatment? It is not a matter of just pushing for a specific statute but to push for passage of all statutes needed to bring the state to 100-percent equality.

Here is what needs to be done in these eighteen states and DC (listed by rating and alphabetical within the same rating):

CALIFORNIA (92%)

With a scorecard rating of 92 percent, California is only missing converting its domestic partnership statute into full marriage (as it was in 2008, until Proposition 8 passed). The matter is expected to be resolved by the Supreme Court in June 2013.

In the meantime, the California legislature (controlled by the Democrats) and the Democratic governor have led the nation in passing legislation for equality, including teaching the historical contributions of LGBT people in history (many of these people are highlighted in Appendix 1).

DISTRICT OF COLUMBIA (92%)

The key goal missing is the treatment of birth certificates for transgender people. The Washington, DC Council should be able to address this without any problem as they ask: what else is missing to ensure that our LGBT residents are fully equal under the law in DC?

NEW JERSEY (92%)

The main goal pending is converting civil unions into marriages. The legislature passed such a law in 2012, but it was vetoed by Republican Governor Chris Christie, who is up for reelection in November 2013.

State leaders are considering three strategies to win full equality: (1) persuade more legislators to vote for marriage equality and overturn the governor's veto, (2) take it to a popular vote, or (3) present a new case (*Garden State Equality v. Dow*) to the New Jersey Supreme Court, which ruled unanimously in 2006 that New Jersey had to provide the same rights, benefits, and responsibilities to all couples, whether they are the same gender or not. However, it did not require civil marriage.

IOWA (92%)

This is one of the pioneering states for equality in our country—not just for LGBT rights. In 2012, Democrats maintained their majority in the Senate, and a state Supreme Court justice who voted for marriage equality was retained despite a fierce campaign against him; both actions suggest that marriage equality is safe for the moment in Iowa.

To reach full LGBT legal equality, Iowa is only missing a statute to handle parenting rights (adoption) for LGBT people. However, with a Republican governor and assembly, to go the last mile will require some work.

COLORADO (83%)

After shifting the legislature to Democratic control and having a Democratic governor, Colorado is very likely to pass civil unions legislation soon—it actually did as this book went to press. Marriage is currently forbidden by a constitutional amendment. It should also address any inequalities for transgender people (especially related to amended birth certificates). These changes would bring the state from a current rating of 83 percent to 92 percent. To go the final mile to full equality would require rescinding the state's constitutional amendment against same-gender marriage.

ILLINOIS (83%)

This state could go to full equality by taking two actions:

1. Changing civil unions to full marriage equality.

2. Modifying the state's hate-crime bill to cover gender identity and expression (it already covers sexual orientation).

MASSACHUSETTS (83%)

Massachusetts could easily provide 100-percent legal equality to its LGBT residents by accomplishing two simple tasks for a legislature with a supermajority of Democrats and a governor who is a big supporter of equality:

1. Add protection in public accommodations for gender identity and expression to its nondiscrimination statute.

2. Add gender identity and expression to its anti-bullying statute.

We should push for these changes to occur in 2013 since next year there will be a gubernatorial race that may change the dynamics.

NEW YORK (83%)

After the bipartisan victory for marriage equality in the state in 2011, New York rates at 83 percent and can reach 100 percent if it achieves a couple of long-sought goals:

1. Add gender identity and expression to the existing nondiscrimination statutes regarding employment, housing, credit, and public accommodations.

2. Add gender identity and expression to the state's hate-crime statute, which already covers sexual orientation.

WASHINGTON (83%)

Emboldened by the victory of the popular vote supporting marriage equality, and with a very supporting governor, state house, and state senate, Washington could pass in short order the statutes to provide full legal equality to its LGBT residents:

1. Equal treatment of birth certificates for transgender people. Currently, this is done by policy; it should be by statute.

2. Ensure that the three types of adoption (single, joint, and second-parent) are available to LGBT people who want to be parents. Currently, this is a common practice but it is not done by statute.

Washington is an example of a state that is already doing the right things; it just needs to codify them in statutes.

MAINE (75%)

After the tremendous victory in the popular vote for marriage equality in November 2012, Maine has used the momentum to complete the task for full equality. Only three key items are missing:

1. Add gender identity and expression to the hate-crime statute that already covers sexual orientation.

2. Treat transgender people equally (especially missing is the treatment of birth certificates).

3. Add second-parent adoption.

With a state House and Senate controlled by the Democrats, it should be possible to pass this legislation. Note, however, that the governor is a Republican.

MARYLAND (75%)

Like Maine, this state passed marriage equality by popular vote and has a similar gap to achieve full LGBT legal equality. However, Maryland has the advantage of having a governor eager to please in search of a national spotlight to run for president and a House of Delegates and senate with an overwhelming Democratic majority. Here is what needs to be done:

1. Add gender identity and expression to nondiscrimination statutes for employment, housing, credit, and public accommodations.

2. Treat transgender people equally (especially missing is the treatment of birth certificates).

3. Ensure, by statute, that LGBT people can become parents by allowing these three types of adoption: single, joint, and second-parent.

OREGON (75%)

With a shift in the legislature in the 2012 election, Oregon now has a Democratic governor and Democratic control of the state house and senate. In addition, the new speaker of the state House, Tina Kotek, is openly lesbian. This is what needs to be done:

1. Pass marriage equality by reversing the constitutional amendment, either by popular vote or the courts.

2. Change birth certificates for transgender people to indicate the correct gender.

3. Ensure, by statute, that LGBT people can become parents by allowing these three types of adoption: single, joint, and second-parent.

HAWAII (67%)

With a governor, house, and senate all fully Democratic, this state should do a big push for LGBT equality. Two of the items missing could be done with relative ease. The third one is more difficult:

1. Pass anti-bullying legislation that covers sexual orientation and gender identity and expression.

2. Ensure, by statute, that LGBT people can become parents by allowing these three types of adoption: single, joint, and second-parent.

3. Change civil unions into full marriage equality. This would need, however, a popular vote or court ruling to change the state constitution (which was amended in 1998).

MINNESOTA (67%)

With a shift in the composition of the legislature and a victory defeating a constitutional amendment, both in the 2012 elections, Minnesota is poised for bringing full LGBT equality to its residents. Here is what needs to be done:

1. Pass marriage equality.

2. Change birth certificates for transgender people as a matter of statute as opposed to the current system, which depends on the courts.

3. Ensure, by statute, that LGBT people can become parents by allowing these three types of adoption: single, joint, and second-parent.

NEW HAMPSHIRE (67%)

With a new Democratic governor, a state house of representatives with an ample Democratic majority, and a state senate with a slight thirteen-to-eleven Republican majority, New Hampshire can finish the job of providing full LGBT equality. The heavy lifting has already been done by passing civil unions and later same-gender marriage. This is what is missing:

1. Add gender identity and expression to the hate-crime statute that already includes sexual orientation.

2. Add gender identity and expression to the statues for non discrimination in employment, housing, credit, and public accommodations (which already include sexual orientation).

3. Ensure that birth certificates indicate the correct gender for transgender people.

4. Ensure, by statute, that LGBT people can become parents by allowing these three types of adoption: single, joint, and second-parent.

NEW MEXICO (67%)

This is a state with Democratic majorities in the state house and senate, but with a Republican governor. Here is what is missing for full LGBT legal equality:

1. Marriage equality legislation—the state already recognizes marriages from other states. New Mexico does not have a constitutional amendment limiting marriage to a man and a woman.

2. Anti-bullying legislation specifying sexual orientation and gender identity and expression.

3. Ensure, by statute, that LGBT people can become parents by allowing these three types of adoption: single, joint, and second-parent.

DELAWARE (50%)

This is a state with a Democratic governor and Democratic state house and senate. Here is what needs to be accomplished:

1. Add gender identity and expression to the hate-crime statute (which already covers sexual orientation).

2. Add gender identity to the nondiscrimination statute.

3. Provide same-gender marriage (it has now civil unions).

4. Create an anti-bullying statute covering sexual orientation and gender identity and expression.

5. Ensure, by statute, that LGBT people can become parents by allowing these three types of adoption: single, joint, and second-parent.

NEVADA (50%)

Admittedly, it will require some work to bring Nevada to 100 percent given that it has a Republican governor, a Democratic assembly, and a senate with a slim Democratic majority (eleven to ten). Here is what needs to be done:

1. Add gender identity and expression to the hate-crime statute (which already covers sexual orientation).

2. Provide marriage equality (the state already has domestic partnerships), but need to overturn the constitutional amendment banning same-gender marriage.

3. Create an anti-bullying statute covering sexual orientation and gender identity and expression.

4. Ensure, by statute, that LGBT people can become parents by allowing these three types of adoption: single, joint, and second-parent.

RHODE ISLAND (50%)

Like Delaware, Rhode Island currently has only a 50-percent rating but can achieve 100 percent given that it has an overwhelming Democratic majority in the state senate and house (with a gay speaker of the house, Gordon Fox) and a governor, Lincoln Chafee, who is an independent and who is totally pro-equality. Here is what needs to be done:

1. Add gender identity and expression to the hate-crime statute (which already covers sexual orientation).

2. Provide marriage equality (already has civil unions).

3. Ensure that birth certificates indicate the correct gender for transgender people.

4. Create an anti-bullying statute covering sexual orientation and gender identity and expression.

5. Ensure, by statute, that LGBT people can become parents by allowing these three types of adoption: single, joint, and second-parent.

How many of these eighteen states (and DC) will reach full LGBT equality in 2013? The time is now for a big push.

What about the other states? Read on.

60.

The Other Thirty States

While two states have achieved full LGBT equality and eighteen others and the District of Columbia could achieve it with a focused push, in the other thirty states, it is more challenging. In most of these thirty states, the conservatives control the governorships and the legislatures. Progress can indeed be made, but it does require creative thinking and new approaches to break through. In the short term, most relief will come from passing federal legislation and through the rulings of the courts. All of these states, except for Indiana, Pennsylvania, West Virginia, and Wyoming, have constitutional amendments defining marriage as between one man and one woman, which will have to be overturned by the courts or popular vote.

These thirty states are: Alabama, Alaska, Arizona, Arkansas, Florida, Georgia, Idaho, Indiana, Kansas, Kentucky, Louisiana, Michigan, Mississippi, Missouri, Montana, Nebraska, North Carolina, North Dakota, Ohio, Oklahoma, Pennsylvania, South Carolina, South Dakota, Tennessee, Texas, Utah, Virginia, West Virginia, Wisconsin, and Wyoming.

Here is the status of each equality goal in these states, as a group.

EQUALITY GOAL: NONDISCRIMINATION

This has been an elusive goal to achieve, despite its having been supported by most Americans and being fundamental for every person's well-being. Without nondiscrimination protections, most people are not able to be out of the closet and be true to who they are or able to contribute to society up to their potential.

Another reality is that, in some more progressive states, the state statutes are stronger than the federal ones. However, conservative states that currently do not have nondiscrimination statutes for sexual orientation and gender identity are not expected to create stronger ones than the proposed federal law.

Of the thirty states in this group, twenty-nine do not offer any nondiscrimination protection for LGBT people. Only one state (Wisconsin) offers protection, but limited to sexual orientation.

Fortunately, transgender people are now protected nationwide against employment discrimination under Title VII of the Civil Rights Act.

EQUALITY GOAL: MARRIAGE EQUALITY

The results here are abysmal: except for Wisconsin, which offers domestic partnerships, none of the other twenty-nine states offers any type of relationship recognition for same-gender couples.

EQUALITY GOAL: PROTECTING YOUTH

Of the thirty states in this group, only North Carolina and West Virginia offer critical anti-bullying legislation with specific enumeration of sexual orientation and gender identity and expression. Wisconsin offers protection based only on sexual orientation. The other states offer nothing.

Research conducted by GLSEN shows that anti-bullying statutes must identify specific groups protected by the legislation, otherwise it is not effective, so we do not count states with generic policies (such as Florida).

EQUALITY GOAL: PARENTING

Parenting and adoption is mostly a state issue and, in most cases, is handled through the courts on a case-by-case basis rather than by statute. Of these states, Indiana is the only one offering the three types of adoption needed for legal equality: (1) a single LGBT person adopting, (2) joint adoption by a same-gender couple, and (3) second-parent adoption by a same-gender couple.

Beyond Indiana, adoption in the other states depends on the jurisdiction within the state, or it has not been tested.

EQUALITY GOAL: FREEDOM OF GENDER

There is a multitude of approaches in these thirty states regarding birth certificates:

- In one state (Indiana), there is no indication of gender in the birth certificate.

- In ten states, a new birth certificate is issued with the new gender.

- In three states (Idaho, Ohio, and Tennessee), the original gender in the birth certificate cannot be changed.

- In three states (Montana, Texas, and Wisconsin), a court or court clerk makes the decision.

- In the rest of the states, the birth certificate is amended (still showing the gender at birth).

EQUALITY GOAL: HATE CRIMES

Since 2009, there has been federal hate crimes legislation which covers sexual orientation and gender identity. This legislation is very useful, but it is not a replacement for hate-crime legislation in the states.

Of the thirty states in our group, only one (Missouri) offers a hate-crime statute covering sexual orientation and gender identity and expression. Nine others offer protection only for sexual orientation. The other twenty offer no protection. There is still a long way to go in many states.

The next chapter asks an important question.

61.

How Much Is Equality Worth to *You?*

Equality doesn't just happen on its own. Many people give substantial amounts of money, time, and talent to make it happen.

The culture of giving is important, regardless of how much money you have. Consider any of the ideas below (or create your own) depending on your financial situation:

1. *Give a few dollars.*
   Most people can donate a few dollars from time to time. No matter how much you can afford, giving helps bring equality.

2. *Give a percentage of your annual income.*
   This is a common formula—for example, give 10 percent of your annual income, as some religious traditions suggest (tithing toward a worthy cause).

3. *Give a percentage of your net assets (or your assets in stock investments).*
   Some experts believe that if you spend less than 4 percent per year of your invested assets, you will not run out of money in your lifetime, and your assets will still keep up with inflation. Of course, this is based on many assumptions, so you need to check with your financial advisor.

4. *Give a percentage of your disposable income.*
   Deduct from your income your basic expenses: taxes, mortgage, and basic living expenses. Then give a small part of what's left to advance equality.

5. *Give a part of your annual bonus.*
   In their minds, people do not count bonuses as part of regular income. So why not use part of it to obtain your legal rights (for example, to ensure that you or cannot be fired solely for your sexual orientation of gender identity)?

A SIMPLE GIVING PLAN

There are many causes that deserve your money, but if you or someone you love is lesbian, gay, bisexual, or transgender, why not give first to promote fundamental fairness?

It is easy to create a giving plan. Start by considering three main buckets in which to put your money:

1. Amount you want to give in the next twelve months to advance LGBT equality: $_____

2. Amount you want to give in the next twelve months to other LGBT issues: $_____

3. Amount you want to give in the next twelve months to non-LGBT issues: $_____

For the amount that you want to give to advance equality (first bucket), consider the following split:

- 40 percent for politicians and political organizations that will assist in passing legislation for equality (in election years, maybe this should be 60 percent);

- 40 percent for nonprofits working to achieve equality (in election years, maybe this should be 30 percent);

- 10 percent for opportunity giving (in election years, maybe this is reduced to 5 percent); and

- 10 percent for social-obligations giving (in election years, maybe reduce to 5 percent)

These percentages are just a guideline. Modify them to suit your interests, but it is important to stick to an allocation that makes sense for you and your interests.

A culture of giving will do wonders for your spirit and, combined with the donations of other people, will lead to change.

If you have the financial means, the next chapter is for you—otherwise, just skip it.

62.

Strategic and Creative Donors

Advances in equality have occurred because of the dedication and sacrifices of many grassroots volunteers, elected officials, and staff people working for nonprofits and many people fortunate enough (and generous enough) to fund the movement.

This chapter focuses on big donors. It discusses fourteen different strategies they can follow for their giving.

There are many terms used to describe strategic philanthropy: intelligent giving, strategic giving, effective philanthropy, venture philanthropy, inspired philanthropy. Donors, especially mega donors, create a unique combination of strategies that best fit their needs—for more details on these strategies, including online resources, please check www.eQualityGiving.org/Giving-Center.

1. IMPACT GIVING

Donors concentrate their giving on a few organizations, political candidates, or equality goals with *large* donations that have a significant impact.

Good for:

- Donors with large budgets
- Donors with solid strategic visions that can change the movement

2. ORGANIZATIONAL GIVING

Donors concentrate most of their giving on a single organization.

Good for:

- Members of the board of that organization, as well as its senior employees
- Donors whose professional interests match the organization direction (e.g., an attorney giving to a legal defense organization)

3. GOAL GIVING

Donors concentrate their giving on achieving an equality goal instead of on an organization.

Good for:

- Donors passionate to achieve specific equality goals (e.g., protecting youth or marriage equality)
- Donors who are very strategic and have a passion for specific equality goals

4. CONCENTRATED GIVING

Donors give to a limited number of organizations and political candidates.

Good for:

- Donors with more limited budgets

5. DISPERSED GIVING

In this strategy, donors give to a multitude of organizations and political candidates.

Good for:

- Donors with large budgets
- Donors who have a hard time saying no

- Donors who fundraise for other causes—this approach creates goodwill among donors who support each other's causes.

6. OPPORTUNITY GIVING

Donors give to take advantage of an immediate opportunity that will achieve a tangible result in a short time (usually a year or less).

Good for:

- Donors who want to see immediate results

7. CAPACITY GIVING

Donors give to build the capacity of an organization or political party and make them more robust over a long time.

Good for:

- Donors who know and trust the senior leadership of the organization and believe in the potential of its mission

8. LOCAL GIVING

Donors give to organizations and politicians in their local communities and states.

Good for:

- Donors who want to make a tangible difference in the lives of their communities
- Donors who want to get to know and influence their local and state politicians

9. MAVERICK GIVING

Donors who want to give to unconventional causes or lesser-known organizations/politicians.

Good for:

- Donors who like to create new paths

10. ANGEL GIVING

Donors who give to help new organizations get established.

Good for:

- Donors interested in social entrepreneurship

11. GAP GIVING

Donors review each of the equality goals and each of the strategic approaches to achieve LGBT equality and give to the areas that are insufficiently funded.

Good for:

- Donors with considerable financial means
- Donors interested in strategic analysis

12. COLLABORATIVE GIVING

Donors give jointly with other donors in the pursuit of a common goal. Examples of this approach are giving circles and some foundations. There are two flavors to collaborative giving: (1) donors give to a fund and a committee distributes the money; or (2) donors are presented with a set of options, and they decide individually how much to give to each of the options.

Good for:

- Donors sharing common passions
- Donors who do not have the time or interest in researching the potential grantees by themselves

13. CONVEYOR GIVING

Donors decide on a goal to be achieved and search for the proper organizations or groups to help achieve it jointly. Donors, in effect, convey a group of organizations and people for a joint goal.

Good for:

- Donors with significant giving capabilities
- Donors respected by the groups that they are conveying
- Donors with the time and abilities to bring together different groups

14. SOCIAL GIVING

Donors give based on social obligations and requests from friends.

Good for:

- Donors who do not want to say no

If you are a big donor, you can use one or more of the strategies presented to maximize the impact of your giving, taking into account your personal situation.

The next chapter will show how to apply these donor strategy ideas to supporting LGBT organizations.

63.

Your Turn: Supporting Organizations

This chapter is for people who are (or want to become) donors to organizations for equality. Before you think about supporting an organization, think about which equality goal you are most passionate about. Is it marriage? Is it employment nondiscrimination? Is it freedom of gender? Or another one? Then reread the chapter of this book in Part II that discusses that goal. You will see mentioned there good organizations whose missions are aligned with that goal. Of course, there are other good organizations (especially at the state level) that may not be mentioned in this book.

Another approach is to focus on the paths to reach equality instead of a specific equality goal. These paths are discussed in Part III of this book. Focusing on a path is very appropriate if you have a specialty that matches it. For instance, if you are an attorney, your focus may not be on a single goal but to reach equality through the courts.

If your focus is religion, check organizations focused on this, such as the InterfaithAlliance.org and the ReligiousInstitute.org. For a different perspective on religion, check FaithInAmerica.org.

When giving to nonprofit organizations, consider these tips:

- *Give for multiple years*
  Some people recommend three-year commitments, but your commitment should be until a specific goal is reached.

- *Give consistently*
  In election years, it is very tempting to give more for political issues at the expense of the nonprofits. Organizations need stability, so continue supporting them despite the notion that this might be the "election of a lifetime."

- *Check outcomes*
  What has the organization achieved each year for equality?
  How relevant is this to achieving legal equality? Does the
  organization have a written plan with the specific goals to be
  achieved that year?

- *Help with unplanned opportunities*
  In a perfect world, organizations would know what they are
  going to do for the whole year. In reality, new funding may
  be required to take advantage of a new opportunity. For
  example, an organization may need extra money to fund a
  survey on a new development. This is not an excuse for
  organizations that not plan properly. It is helpful to be there
  for well-managed organizations that want to make the best
  of a new situation.

- *Ask more*
  The organizations that you support should think big and act
  differently. They should have a governing board that is fully
  inclusive of our community, including transgender people.

For the next chapter, let's turn our attention to specific actions you
can take to support equality in 2013.

64.

Your Turn: Ten Actions *You* Can Take *Now*

"Individual involvement and grassroots action are
paramount to success and must be encouraged."

—The Dallas Principles,
Principle #6

You want more ideas of what to do in 2013? Here are ten actions.
Choose those that are more appropriate for you.

1. HELP WIN IN THE SUPREME COURT

In June 2013, the Supreme Court will decide two critical
cases for LGBT equality. You can help in two ways.

First, support the American Foundation for Equal Rights
(AFER.org) and the American Civil Liberties Union LGBT
Project (ACLU.org/lgbt-rights); they are the organizations
defending the cases, and such litigation is very expensive.

Second, support creative actions to highlight our need for
legal equality, especially in the first half of 2013—this may
have an effect on the Supreme Court.

2. DEMAND FULL EQUALITY NOW

The time for delays and excuses is over. We will never get
full equality if we do not ask for it. Whether you are an
insider or an outsider, demand full equality now from the
president (executive orders, appointments, etc.), Congress,
the state legislatures, and the courts. As Dr. Martin Luther
King, Jr., said, *"A right delayed is a right denied."*

For federal legislation, review the Equality & Religious Freedom Act (Omnibus Equality Bill) written by Karen Doering, Esq., and introduced by eQualityGiving on March 18, 2009 (www.eQualityGiving.org/Blueprint-for-LGBT-Equality).

We need federal legislation that is comprehensive and does not negotiate away our equal rights even before it is introduced. Ask Representative Jared Polis to introduce such legislation instead of a compendium of existing bills.

Follow up with the status of pro-equality federal legislation on www.ActOnPrinciples.org.

3. HELP WIN IN THE STATES

The good news is that we are fully equal under the law in two states (Vermont and Connecticut). The bad news is that we are unequal in 96 percent of the states. Check here where your state stands:
www.eQualityGiving.org/States-of-Equality-and-Gay-Rights-Scorecard

With some work, we can soon convert eighteen other states and the District of Columbia to full equality. See the details in Chapter 58 and then help. In the other thirty states, it is tougher, but that also means there is more opportunity to have a significant impact; check the details in Chapter 59.

4. DO MAKE IT BETTER FOR OUR YOUTH

After the heart-rending "It Gets Better" campaign by Dan Savage, the issue is how we can *make* it better for our youth *now*. This is a topic that you need to bring up at every town hall meeting for Republicans and Democrats alike.

5. CREATE DIALOG ABOUT RELIGION'S ROLE

Reread Part I of this book to be prepared for discussions with family, coworkers, and friends about the freedom of religion. Remember that most religious leaders do not want politicians *to use religion as an excuse for their legislative actions.*

6. BUILD BRIDGES WITH CORPORATE AMERICA

One of the new challenges after the *Citizens United* decision is that a corporation may give a grant to your favorite LGBT organization while at the same time secretly donating to elect legislators who do not support our equality under the law. One of the significant gaps in our movement, and for electoral transparency, is that we do not have a database of corporate giving to politicians and candidates. This is not easy to do without legislation requiring disclosure of donors, but it is critical. If you have ties to corporations as an executive, employee, or shareholder, you can push for limiting corporate involvement to candidates who do not harm equality.

7. ENSURE GOVERNANCE WITH FULL LGBT REPRESENTATION

The board of directors that governs the LGBT organizations need to fully represent the movement. Work with the boards and executive directors of the organizations with which you are involved to ensure full representation. There is particular need of more transgender board members. Thirteen of our largest national LGBT organizations do not have a single transgender board member. Check this transgender board member resource:
www.eQualityGiving.org/Transgender-Board-Members

Also, you can listen to this prominent panel about the perils of tokenism: www.eQualityGiving.org/eQualityThinking-The-T-in-LGBTQ

So, ask any organization that you support with your money or time to have a fully representative governing board.

8. BE A DONOR (SMALL OR LARGE)

If you have never given for equality, consider giving to the organizations mentioned in this book. Or give to fund projects using crowd funding, in which many people give small amounts to projects sponsored by organizations, companies, or individuals—check GetGayFunded.com. Support organizations that think bigger and act differently, as well as new organizations and creative individuals with new ideas. Check Chapters 61 and 62 for ideas.

We all get comfortable with a certain level and way of giving. We all need to stretch more and be more generous, but also be bolder and take more risks. A good site to check out is BolderGiving.org and, for specific information on LGBT donors check, eQualityGiving.org, as well as Funders for LGBTQ Issues, LGBTFunders.org.

If you are a donor with contacts with major foundations, point out the leadership of the Ford Foundation, which, in November 2012, announced a five-year $50-million effort fighting for the rights of LGBT people.

9. DO SOMETHING ABOUT HIV CRIMINALIZATION

Some of the most insidious laws against anyone with HIV involve criminalizing HIV. Even very well-informed people may not fully realize the effect of these laws nationally and internationally.

10. THINK REALLY BIG AND DIFFERENTLY

Don't be limited by mediocrity slogans such as *"Politics is the art of the possible."* Don't stop action because it is not possible to pass legislation in a Republican House of Representatives. Think creatively about how to further highlight our inequality now that we are in front of the Supreme Court.

65.

Your Turn, Your Way

So many equality goals, so many paths to reach equality, so many priorities, so many actions you can take. How do you choose?

Choose your goal based on your *passion*.

Choose your path based on your *skills*.

If you have the passion, the skills, and the proper resources for the task (money or time), you can push for equality your own way—without following the established paths.

For example, in September 2010, Dan Savage created, basically single-handedly, the important campaign "It Gets Better." Within two months, President Obama and many others in his administration had produced a video to tell LGBT youth that it gets better.

Here's one more example: a donor friend saw a need in his town to help LGBT high school seniors have their own prom so they could be themselves. He made it happen for fifteen hundred dollars. It has been among the most satisfying cases of giving in his (generous) life as a philanthropist.

Here's a final example: another friend studied the new restrictive registration laws in Florida and determined ways to comply with them at a minimum cost so that the maximum number of people could be registered. His efforts made a difference in 2012 in this critical battleground state.

So, how do you go about going your own way?

Consider these four approaches:

1. *The Highway*
   In this approach, you go through an established organization

(maybe you are on its board or are a volunteer or donor). Here are the steps that you follow:

1. Have an idea
2. Discuss the idea
3. Present the idea to the board
4. Improve the idea based on feedback
5. Get approval for the idea
6. Fundraise to pay for it
7. Do it!

2. *The Shortcut*
   Here, you just do it yourself—no bureaucracies.
   1. Have an idea
   2. Do it!

   This works very well if you are a very creative person and just use standard (and free) tools such as Facebook, Twitter, YouTube, blogs, and others.

3. *The Expert's Way*
   In this case, you become an expert (for example, in election law) and help make a big step forward for equality. This method requires talent and much patience since it is very time-consuming. But it is priceless.

4. *No Road*
   In the ultimate freedom, you decide not to follow any of the paths above. Just do some constant random acts that move us closer to equality. Be creative. The dots will connect one day.

If you can go on your own path and are very creative, you can have a very significant impact. Remember Apple's commercial quoted at the beginning of Part IV of this book:

> "Here's to the crazy ones, the misfits, the rebels, the troublemakers, the round pegs in the square holes... because the people who are crazy enough to think that they can change the world are the ones that do."

Is this you? It certainly is *me*. The next chapter presents my own path.

66.

My Turn, My Way

This book is not about theories about equality, it is all based on things that I have done myself.

The path I chose for equality was very simple. First, identify what the goals are (I created the term *equality goals*). Second, determine the steps required to achieve those goals. Third, create the tools to make this a reality.

In summary, gaining equality under the law is all about creating the intellectual framework of what needs to be done and then creating the tools to do it. In reality, I am a tool creator. These tools help accelerate reaching equality.

So here is what this is all about in more detail:

1. IMMEDIATE GOAL: EQUAL UNDER THE LAW

We should not confuse legal equality with social justice or equality in real terms. The immediate and necessary goal is to reach equality under the law.

TOOL CREATED: Equality Goals
By comparing the protections of what other groups have and the LGBT people do not have, it is easy to set the equality goals—the protections under the law that we are missing. These goals are explained in detail in Part II of this book.

TOOL CREATED: eQualityGiving.org website
This website is focused on how donors can accelerate achieving LGBT legal equality. It is organized based on the equality goals. All other major LGBT organizations arrange their websites by issues (which are very different from goals).

2. EQUALITY GOALS IN LEGAL TERMS

Once you have the equality goals, it is important to write them in legal terms so that they can be enacted as legislation.

TOOLS CREATED: Omnibus Equality Bill and American Equality Bill
These tools serve to tell legislators: this is what we want—no more, no less than other groups. This *is* the gay agenda.

These proposed bills also serve as model bills so that, even if legislation is introduced affecting only one part that is covered in the omnibus bill, it serves as a reference in case that bill gets watered down before passage. This legislation was written at my request by Karen M. Doering, Esq., a great lawyer specializing in nondiscrimination law.

The American Equality Bill, championed by J. Todd Fernandez, Esq., is the subset of the omnibus bill that focuses on adding the terms *sexual orientation* and *gender identity* to the Civil Rights Act.

3. STRATEGY TO REACH THE EQUALITY GOALS

Once we have identified the equality goals, it is easy to determine the basic strategy. Which goals are better addressed in states and which ones at the federal level? What's the priority? What's the investment required?

TOOL CREATED: Strategic Matrices
These matrices address the questions above in a clear manner. They are available at
www.eQualityGiving.org/Giving-to-Charity-Guide.

TOOL CREATED: Discussion Network
A network of major and mega donors, executive directors of LGBT organizations, pro-equality elected officials and endorsed candidates, and thought leaders who discuss how to achieve LGBT equality.

4. CANDIDATE ENDORSEMENT

Because the main objective is to be equal under the law,

candidate endorsements are very important—since candidates are the future legislators who will vote for our equality.

TOOLS CREATED: Endorsement Framework and Endorsed Candidates List
The framework and the endorsement criteria are unique: www.eQualityGiving.org/Endorsements.

This framework is used for actual endorsements in which every candidate submits a questionnaire that can be made public and is personally interviewed (with the exception of President Obama, with whom I spoke but not in a formal endorsement interview): www.eQualityGiving.org/Endorsed-Candidates.

5. FOLLOW THROUGH

After the elections, it is very important to follow through and ensure that legislation is being introduced, voted on, and passed.

Is a bill ready to be voted on? How many votes do we have? To answer these questions, the leadership of the House and Senate conduct whip counts, in which they poll members of their own parties about their positions on a piece of legislation. Whip counts are also conducted at the state level. Lobbyists conduct their own whip counts (although usually partially, since it is very labor-intensive).

TOOL CREATED: ActOnPrinciples.org
This is a unique tool that makes whip counts public and allows a registered user to update the whip count. There is nothing like it anywhere else. The tool is kept up-to-date by Donald Hitchcock.

TOOL CREATED: Platform for Other Contributors
By creating a versatile platform, specific web pages can be created very quickly that allow others to lead important projects. For example:

1. Andrew Tobias, treasurer of the Democratic National Committee, created and keeps updated the most comprehensive list

available of accomplishments by the administration and Congress on LGBT equality:
www.eQualityGiving.org/Accomplishments-by-the-Administration-and-Congress-on-LGBT-Equality.

2. Ret. Captain Tom Carpenter, Esq., created the list of issues pending after the repeal of "Don't Ask, Don't Tell":
www.eQualityGiving.org/DADT.

3. Dr. Dana Beyer leads the project to have more transgender board members so that the governance of our organizations represent the full spectrum of LGBT:
www.eQualityGiving.org/Transgender-Board-Members.

6. MEASURE PROGRESS

Once you have clear goals, it is imperative to measure progress.

TOOL CREATED: Federal LGBT Legal Equality Index
It is available here:
www.eQualityGiving.org/Equal-Protection-of-the-Law.

TOOL CREATED: States of Equality Scorecard
This includes an evaluation of every state based on the equality goals; it can be sorted by state, by score, and by goal. It is available here:
www.eQualityGiving.org/States-of-Equality-and-Gay-Rights-Scorecard.

7. THINK BIGGER, ACT DIFFERENTLY—URGENCY

We need a constant sense of urgency to achieve the equality goals. Because too many people are suffering, legal equality is needed right now. To do so, the movement needs to think bigger and act differently.

TOOL CREATED: THE DALLAS PRINCIPLES
I convened the meeting of twenty-four leaders who created

the Dallas Principles, which is described in detail in Chapter 31 and Appendix 2 of this book and is also available online: www.TheDallasPrinciples.com.

TOOL CREATED: eQualityThinking
This was a unique conference, described here: www.eQualityThinking.org.

TOOL CREATED: Loving Everywhere.
A request for people to send their pictures and letters to the Supreme Court justices, explaining the practical need for same-gender marriages to be valid and recognized everywhere: www.LovingEverywhere.com.

8. THIS SERIES OF BOOKS

This should be a useful tool since it is intended to be a comprehensive guide to reach legal equality for the LGBT community. Like any good guidebook is updated annually to include the specific actions to take that year.

The final tool mentioned is this book. It includes all my prior work and expands on it—not only the content, but addressing a wider audience. Achieving legal equality is not only important for LGBT people and their allies but for all persons who—independent of their religion or political affiliation—believe in the equality expressed in the United States Constitution and Declaration of Independence.

67.

Summary: All In

After the electoral victories in 2012 for LGBT equality, 2013 is clearly a tipping point with two cases in front of the Supreme Court.

This is not a year to sit on the sidelines. First, it is critical to immediately support the two organizations leading the expensive fight in the Supreme Court: the ACLU and AFER. Second, it is time to be creative with actions that will show the Supreme Court the importance of our legal equality. Third, it is important to bring as many Republicans into the cause of equality under the law as possible.

Choose your own path to help. You may have time but no cash—then volunteer. You may have cash and no time—then give.

Do whatever fits your means, time, personality, passion, and skills. The more you can think bigger and act differently, the better.

This is not the time for delays or excuses. This is not the time for outmoded clichés such as *"politics is the art of the possible."* In reality, *politics is the art of leadership.* This is the time for insiders to publicly push for full equality now. This is the time for the president to be our fiercest public advocate. This is the time for Congress and state legislatures to make true the promise of equality under the law. This is also the time for Republicans to join in the promise of equality in our Declaration of Independence and Constitution.

A Respectful Message for *You*

- **To President Obama:** *This is your opportunity as a fierce advocate.*
  There is one simple goal: LGBT people treated equally under the law. No delays. No excuses.

- **To legislators:** *Equality under the law is what makes the United States of America a great country.*
  Every day that you delay enacting equality legislation, you are affecting real people, and you are not complying with your oath of office.

- **To a religious person:** *Protect your freedom of religion.*
  Your freedom of religion is only possible if others have freedom of religion. This means that we cannot write civil laws based on any particular religion.

- **To parents and grandparents:** *You determine what your family's values are.*
  Do you love your children equally? Do you treat them equally? Do you want others to do the same?

- **To teenagers:** *Bullying is not cool.*
  Bullies are immature, cruel, and insecure. Definitely not cool.

- **To LGBT teenagers:** *We will make it better.*
  Teenage years are always difficult—more difficult because of the immature bullies. Truly, it gets better. And a bunch of us are working hard every day to make it better now.

- **To bullies:** *We know your game.*
  You might be an immature and cruel teenage bully, not understanding the harmful effects that bullying has on somebody's life. Or you might be an adult political bully, intentionally misleading people about what family values are, what freedom of religion entails, or what the Constitution really means and, in doing so, harming the lives

of many people. But we Americans now know your game and will stand up to protect our Constitution, our family values, our individualism, our freedom of religion, and our unalienable right to happiness. *Game over.*

Epilogue: The Ultimate Goal

The gay agenda is simply to fulfill the American promise to treat every individual equally under the law—independently of their sexual orientation (heterosexual, homosexual, or bisexual) or their gender identity or expression. So it affects every person.

Imagine living in a country in which:

- Each of us is respected and has an opportunity to develop to our maximum capacity.

- Each of us can pursue happiness on our own terms.

- A religion's laws—whether from Bahai, Buddhism, Christianity, Hinduism, Islam, Judaism, Mormonism, or others—are not imposed on non-members.

- The courts are truly independent.

- Each of us is judged by our actions and not prejudged because of the color of our skin, our gender, our race, our national origin, our disability, our religion, our sexual orientation, or our gender identity or expression.

This country already exists, and it is bound by a great Constitution and inscribed in the façade of the Supreme Court building: Equal Under Law.

What needs to be done is known. Time is of the essence because the current unequal treatment causes real damage to real people. So, let's work for:

Full legal equality now. No delays. No excuses.

As you know from reading this book, full equality under the law is the next step, but what is the ultimate goal?

The ultimate goal is a world without prejudice.

As Mother Theresa said: "If you judge people, you have no time to love them."

The irony is that, on one hand, achieving a world without prejudice is a very difficult goal to reach. On the other hand, it can be reached because each of us has the power to stop prejudging others *right now*.

May we all become inspired and live without prejudice.

Thank *You!*

Countless people engaged daily in achieving equality for the LGBT community have influenced the thoughts expressed in this book and in the eQualityGiving website (where parts of this book appeared first).

These people include the authors of the Dallas Principles; all the members of the Discussion Network of eQualityGiving; the eighty-two panelists and twenty-seven question moderators of eQualityThinking; the webmaster, editors, and champions of Act On Principles; the elected officials eQualityGiving has endorsed over the years; the speakers and participants at OutGiving; and the executive directors and staff of equality organizations who work so hard to achieve equality.

Thanks to my editor, Doreen Space, and to the kind people who endured reading a draft of this manuscript or key parts of it and provided comments: Dana Beyer, MD, James Esseks, Esq,, Stephen Herbits, Esq., Michael Krawitz, Esq., and Janice Langbehn, MS.

For more than anybody else, my appreciation and love is for Dr. Ken Ahonen-Jover. He is my soul mate, best friend, sounding board, and spouse.

About the Author

Juan Ahonen-Jover, Ph.D., is an entrepreneur who did well and is now doing good. He is the creator and cofounder of eQualityGiving, ActOnPrinciples, eQualityThinking, and Loving Everywhere and the convener of the Omnibus Bill and the Dallas Principles—all focused on the fundamental principle that everyone should be treated equally under the law.

Juan was awarded a Fulbright fellowship and was educated at Stanford University in supercomputers and business. He has four advanced degrees and is fluent in four languages. He co-authored a book on computers and is an innovator in election protection.

Juan enjoys speaking engagements from time to time. Contact him at www.GayAgenda2013.com.

APPENDIX 1:

Notable LGBT People

This appendix lists a few lesbian, gay, bisexual, and transgender people (LGBT) who are particularly notable. The list is not comprehensive, by any means. We cannot understand the gay agenda without knowing some of the LGBT figures and their contributions to society.

How do we know that these people are gay, lesbian, bisexual, or transgender? Some cases are easy since the person publicly announced his or her sexual orientation or gender identity. For others, there is plenty of historical evidence, while still others are more disputed. If you want to learn more about their contributions to society or their coming out status, Wikipedia has good write-ups about them.

POLITICS AND GOVERNMENT

- **Johanna Sigurdardottir** (1942–). Lesbian. Current Prime Minister of Iceland since 2009.

- **Elio di Rupo** (1951–). Gay. Prime Minister of Belgium since 2011.

- **Per-Kristina Foss** (1950–). Gay. Prime Minister of Norway for a brief period in 2002,.

- **Guido Westerwelle** (1961–). Gay. Vice Chancellor of Germany (2009–2011). Foreign Minister of Germany since 2009.

- **Bertrand Delanoe** (1950–). Gay. Current Mayor of Paris since 2001.

- **Klaus Wowereit** (1953–). Gay. Current Mayor of Berlin since 2001.

- **Annise Parker** (1956–). Lesbian. Current Mayor of Houston since 2010.

- **Christine Quinn** (1966–). Lesbian. Speaker of New York City Council.

- **Tammy Baldwin** (1962–). Lesbian. First female elected from Wisconsin to the US Congress, first openly LGBT person elected to the US House of Representatives (1999–2013), and first openly LGBT person elected to the US Senate (2013–).

- **Barney Frank** (1940–). Gay. Member of the US House of Representatives (1981–2013). Chairman, House Financial Services Committee (2007–2011). First member of Congress to marry a same-gender spouse (2012).

- **Jared Polis** (1975–). Gay. Member of the US House of Representatives (2009–).

- **David Cicilline** (1961–). Gay. Member of the US House of Representatives (2011–).

- **Sean Patrick Maloney** (1966–). Gay. Member of the US House of Representatives (2013–).

- **Mark Pocan** (1964–). Gay. Member of the US House of Representatives (2013–).

- **Mark Takano** (1960–). Gay. Member of the US House of Representatives (2013–).

- **Kyrsten Sinema** (1976–). Bisexual. Member of the US House of Representatives (2013–). First out bisexual elected to Congress.

- **Gerry Studds** (1937–2011). Gay. First Member of Congress to come out while in office.

- **Harvey Milk** (1930–1978). Gay. Member of San Francisco Board of Supervisors, who was murdered along with Mayor Moscone by a fellow supervisor.

- **Nancy Wechsler** (1950–). Lesbian. First open LGBT person elected to office in the United States (Ann Arbor City Council, 1972).

- **Waheed Alli** (1964–). Gay. Muslim. Member of the House of Lords, British Parliament.

- **James McGreevey** (1957–). Gay. Governor of New Jersey (2002–2004).

- **James Hormel** (1933–). Gay. Philanthropist. First openly LGBT ambassador to the United States (Luxembourg, 1999). Appointed during recess (Senate wouldn't confirm him).

- **Michael Guest** (1957–). Gay. US Ambassador to Romania (2001–2004). First openly gay ambassador to be confirmed by Senate. Retired in 2007 in protest for LGBT discrimination in the State Department.

- **J. Edgar Hoover** (1895–1972). Presumed gay. First director of the FBI (1935–1972).

- **Eleanor Roosevelt** (1882–1962). Presumed lesbian. First Lady of the United States (1933–1945).

- **Barbara Jordan** (1936–1996). Lesbian. Member of the US House of Representatives (1973–1979). Leader of the Civil Rights movement.

- **Deborah Batts** (1947–). Lesbian. First openly LGBT person to be appointed as federal judge (1994 by President Clinton).

- **Georgina Beyer** (1957–). Transgender. World's first open transgender individual to be elected to Parliament (New Zealand, 1999).

- **Edward II** (1284–1327). Bisexual. King of England.

- **Frederick the Great** (1712–1786). Presumed gay. King of Prussia (1772–1786).

- **Ferdinand I of Bulgaria** (1861–1948). Bisexual. Tsar of Bulgaria. Declared Bulgaria's independence from the Ottoman Empire.

RELIGION

- **Rev. Troy Perry** (1940–). Gay. Founder, Metropolitan Community Church.

- **Archbishop Carl Bean** (1944–). Gay. Founder, Unity Fellowship Church Movement. Made famous the song "I Was Born This Way" in 1977, well before Lady Gaga.

- **Bishop Gene Robinson** (1947–). Gay. Episcopalian Bishop of New Hampshire—first of any major Christian religion.

- **Bishop Mary Douglas Glasspool** (1954–). Lesbian. First open lesbian to become bishop in the Anglican faith.

- **Rabbi Sharon Kleinbaum** (1959–). Lesbian. Senior Rabbi of the largest LGBT synagogue in the world.

- **Rabbi Stephen Greenberg** (1956–). Gay. First openly gay Orthodox rabbi.

- **Imam Daayiee Adfullah** (1954–). Gay. American Muslim imam. Co-director, Muslims for Progressive Values. Board member, Al-Fatiha Foundation.

- **Irshad Manji** (1968–). Lesbian. Canadian Muslim author, journalist, and advocate. Director of Moral Courage Project and NY University. Books: *Allah, Liberty and Love*; *The Trouble with Islam Today*. Documentary: *Faith Without Fear*

- **John McNeill** (1925–). Gay. Theologian and former Jesuit. Author of multiple books, notably *The Church and the Homosexual* (1976).

- **Rev. Malcolm Boyd** (1923–). Gay. Priest, author of more than thirty books, and civil rights activist. Came out in 1977.

- **Mel White** (1940–). Gay. Clergyman and writer: *Stranger at the Gate; Lust: The Other Side of Love.*

MILITARY

- **Alexander the Great** (356–323 BC). Presumed gay. Emperor, who by age thirty had expanded his domain from Greece to Persia and to Egypt. One of the most successful military commanders of all time.

- **Hadrian** (76–138 AD). Presumed gay. Fourteenth Emperor of the Roman Empire.

- **T. E. Lawrence, "Lawrence of Arabia"** (1888–1935). Presumed gay. Liaison during the Arab Revolt. Writer: *Seven Pillars of Wisdom.*

- **Tammy S. Smith** (1963–). Lesbian. Brigadier General, US Army. First openly LGBT general in the United States military.

SCIENCE

- **Alan Turing** (1912–1954). Gay. Father of computer science and artificial intelligence. Mathematical genius who broke German codes during WWII. His breakthroughs shortened WWII and saved thousands of lives.

- **Baron John Maynard Keynes** (1883–1946). Bisexual. One of the most influential economists ever.

- **Lynn Conway** (1938–). Transgender. Creator of the methodology used to design all computer chips. Also invented method for high-performance computers.

- **Sally Ride** (1951–2012). Lesbian. Astronaut, physicist, engineer, and educator. First American woman in space. Youngest American to go into space (age 32).

- **Nate Silver** (1978–). Gay. Statistician, blogger, author. Accurately predicted the 2008 and 2012 US elections.

- **Joan Roughgarden** (1946–). Transgender. Professor emeritus of biology, Stanford University. Author of eight scientific books.

- **Ben Barres**. Transgender. Chair, Neurobiology, Stanford University School of Medicine.

- **Deirdre McCloskey** (1942–). Transgender. Professor of economics, University of Illinois at Chicago. Author of numerous books.

SPORTS

- **Martina Navratilova** (1956–). Lesbian. Tennis player. All-time career record for men or women in singles and doubles.

- **Greg Louganis** (1960–). Gay. Four Olympic gold medals and five gold World Championships for diving. Best-selling author: *Breaking the Silence*.

- **Mildred "Babe" Zaharias** (1911–1956). Lesbian. One of the greatest athletes of the twentieth century. Two gold and one silver medals in 1932 Olympics. Multitalented: golf, basketball, track and field.

- **Toller Cranston** (1949–). Gay. Figure skater. Canadian national champion. Bronze in 1976 Olympics.

- **Renee Richards** (1934–). Transgender. Ophthalmologist, tennis player, and author.

- **Billie Jean King** (1943–). Lesbian. Professional tennis player.

- **Johnny Weir-Voronov** (1984–). Gay. American figure skater. Three time US national champion.

- **Billy Bean** (1964–). Gay. Former Major League baseball player and author. Came out in 1999. Book: *Going the Other Way*.

- **Glenn Burke** (1952–1995). Gay. Former Major League baseball player. First and only Major League player known to be out to his team while a player.

- **Ian Roberts** (1965–). Gay. First rugby player to come out (1995).

- **John Amaechi** (1974–). Gay. Basketball player.

- **Matthew Mitchman** (1988–). Gay. Olympic Gold for diving (2008) with the highest single-dive score in the history of the Olympics.

- **Sarah Vaillancourt** (1985–). Lesbian. Ice hockey player. Two Olympic gold metals.

- **Rosie Jones** (1959–). Lesbian. Golf player.

- **Ilana Kloss** (1956–). Lesbian. Tennis player. World Team Tennis commissioner.

- **Orlando Cruz** (1981–). Gay. Professional boxer.

BUSINESS

- **Sir Cecil Rhodes** (1853–1902). Presumed gay. Mining magnate. Founder of African state of Rhodesia. Funder of Rhodes scholarships.

- **Tim Cook** (1960–). Gay. CEO of Apple (2011–). One of the highest-paid executives ever ($376 million stock award in 2011).

- **Chris Hughes** (1983–). Gay. Cofounder, Facebook. Owner and publisher, *The New Republic*.

- **Peter Thiel** (1967–). Gay. Entrepreneur, venture capitalist, and hedge fund manager. Early investor in Facebook.

- **Tim Gill** (1953–). Gay. Cofounder of software company Quark. Philanthropist and activist: Gill Foundation and Gill Action, which together invest about $20 million a year to promote equality for LGBT people.

- **David Bohnett** (1956–). Gay. Cofounder of GeoCities, sold to Yahoo in 1999. His foundation has given more than $45 million in grants.

- **Jon Stryker** (1958–). Gay. Billionaire heir to Stryker corporation. Philanthropist.

- **Jonathan Lewis** (1958–). Gay. Progressive Insurance. Investor and visionary philanthropist.

- **Linda Ketner** (1950–). Lesbian. Heir to Food Lion's business. Management consultant and philanthropist.

- **Bruce Bastian** (1948–). Gay. Cofounder, WordPerfect. Philanthropist.

- **Martine Rothblatt** (1954–). Transgender. Attorney, author, and entrepreneur. Founder and CEO, United Therapeutics.

- **Kathy Levinson** (1956–). Lesbian. Former chief operating officer and president, E*Trade. Three-sport varsity athlete. Philanthropist.

- **Megan Smith** (1964–). Lesbian. Vice president, Google.

- **Mitchell Gold**. Gay. Cofounder, Mitchell Gold+Bob Williams furniture. Cofounder, Faith In America. Philanthropist. Author.

- **Bob Page** (1945–). Gay. Founder, Replacements Limited. Philanthropist.

- **Charles Merrill, Jr.** (1920–). Bisexual. Author, artist, and philanthropist. Son of Merrill-Lynch founder.

- **Michael Bishop** (1942–). Gay. Businessperson. Majority owner of BMI airline, which he sold to Lufthansa. Net worth around $800 million.

- **Kevin McClatchy** (1963–). Gay. Businessperson. Principal owner, Pittsburgh Pirates (1996–2007).

LITERATURE AND THEATER

- **William Shakespeare** (1564–1616). Presumed bisexual. Poet and playwright. Considered greatest writer in the English language.

- **Tennessee Williams** (1911–1983). Gay. Writer and playwright: *A Streetcar Named Desire, Cat on a Hot Tin Roof*, and more.

- **Hans Christian Anderson** (1805–1875). Presumed gay. Most famous writer of fairy tales.

- **Walt Whitman** (1819–1892). Gay. Father of free verse. One of the greatest American poets.

- **Virginia Woolf** (1882–1941). Lesbian. Writer: *Mrs. Dalloway, To the Lighthouse, Orlando, A Room of One's Own*, and more.

- **Truman Capote** (1924–1984). Gay. Writer: *Breakfast at Tiffany's, In Cold Blood,* and more.

- **Gore Vidal** (1925–2012). Gay. Writer: *The City and the Pillar, The Best Man, The Last Empire,* and more.

- **André Gide** (1869–1951). Gay. Writer. Literature Nobel Prize, 1947.

- **Ralph Waldo Emerson** (1803–1882). Bisexual. Writer. Leader of the Transcendentalist movement based on self-reliance.

- **E. M. Foster** (1879–1970). Gay. Novelist: *Where Angels Fear to Tread, The Longest Journey, A Room with a View, A Passage to India, Maurice,* and more.

- **Oscar Wilde** (1854–1900). Gay. Playwright and novelist: *The Importance of Being Earnest; Salome, The Picture of Dorian Gray,*

- **Thomas Mann** (1875–1955). Bisexual. Nobel Prize for Literature, 1929. Works: *Buddenbrooks, The Magic*

Mountain, Death in Venice, and more.

- **James Baldwin** (1924–1987). Gay. Writer and civil rights activist. Books: *The Fire Next Time, Go Tell it on the Mountain,* and more.

- **Simone de Beauvoir** (1908–1986). Bisexual. Influential philosopher and writer. Companion of philosopher and author Jean-Paul Sartre.

- **Gertrude Stein** (1874–1946) and **Alice B. Toklas** (1877–1967). Lesbian couple. Writers, art collectors.

- **Dustin Lance Black** (1974–). Gay. Screenwriter. Oscar winner for *Milk* (Best Original Screenplay, 2008).

- **Sir Terence Rattigan** (1911–1977). Gay. Famous British playwright.

- **Harvey Fierstein** (1952–). Gay. Actor and playwright: *Torch Song Trilogy, La Cage aux Folles, A Catered Affair.*

- **Jean Cocteau** (1889–1963). Gay. French writer, artist, and filmmaker. Member: American Academy, French Academy, Royal Academy of Belgium, and German Academy.

- **Federico García Lorca** (1898–1936). Gay. Poet, dramatist, and theater director. One of the most important poets in the Spanish language.

- **Paul Verlaine** (1844–1896). Gay. Renowned French poet.

- **Arthur Rimbaud** (1854–1891). Gay. Prodigy French poet. Had long-term relationship with Paul Verlaine.

- **Armistead Maupin** (1944–). Gay. Writer: *Tales of the City* and more.

- **Alan Ball** (1955–). Gay. Writer, director, actor, producer. *American Beauty* (Oscar for Best Original Screenplay), *Six Feet Under.*

- **Andrew Tobias** (1947–). Gay. Writer about investments, coming out, other topics. Innovator in insurance. Treasurer,

Democratic National Committee.

- **Reinaldo Arenas** (1943–1990). Gay. Best-selling writer of *Before Night Falls, Farewell to the Sea.*

- **W. H. Auden** (1907–1973). Gay. Famous poet.

MUSIC

- **Pyotr Ilyich Tchaikovsky** (1840–1893). Gay. Russian composer of classical music.

- **Leonard Bernstein** (1918–1990). Gay. Renowned American composer and conductor.

- **Sir Elton John** (1947–). Gay. Singer, songwriter, and composer.

- **"Boy George"—George Alan O'Dowd** (1961–). Gay. Singer and songwriter.

- **George Michael** (1963–). Gay. Musician, singer and songwriter.

- **Cole Porter** (1891–1964). Gay. Composer and songwriter. Married Linda Lee Thomas. His parties in Paris were renowned.

- **Joan Baez** (1941–). Bisexual. Folksinger and songwriter.

- **Ricky Martin** (1971–). Gay. Singer and actor.

- **Whitney Houston** (1963–2012). Presumed bisexual. Singer. Actress. The most-awarded female act of all time.

PAINTING, SCULPTURE

- **Leonardo da Vinci** (1452–1519). Presumed gay. Painter, sculptor, architect, scientist, musician, and inventor. One of the greatest geniuses of all time.

- **Michelangelo** (1475–1564). Presumed gay. One of the most famous painters, sculptors, architects, poets, and engineers of the Renaissance.

- **Andy Warhol** (1928–1987). Gay. Artist. Leader of the Pop Art movement.

- **David Hockney** (1937–). Gay. Pop art painter, printmaker, and photographer.

FASHION

- **Cristobal Balenciaga** (1895–1972). Gay. Fashion designer. Founder of the Balenciaga *haute couture* house.

- **Gianni Versace** (1946–1997). Gay. Fashion designer. Founder of the Versace label.

- **Charles Nolan** (1957–2011). Gay. Fashion designer. Founder of the Nolan label.

- **Tom Ford** (1961–). Gay. Fashion designer. Founder of the Ford label. Movie Director: *A Single Man*.

MOVIES, ENTERTAINMENT, TV

- **Rock Hudson** (1925–1985). Gay. Actor who died of AIDS. His movies include: *Magnificent Obsession, Giant, Ice Station Zebra,* and *Dynasty*.

- **Sir Ian McKellen** (1939–). Gay. Actor.

- **George Takei** (1937–). Gay. Actor: *Star Trek*.

- **Angelina Jolie** (1975–). Bisexual. Actress, director, and humanitarian.

- **Rosie O'Donnell** (1962–). Lesbian. TV show host, actress, comedian.

- **Ellen Degeneres** (1958–). Lesbian. Comedian, actress, TV show host.

- **Anderson Cooper** (1967–). Gay. Reporter, author, and TV anchor.

- **Rachel Maddow** (1973–). Lesbian. Author and TV host.

- **Don Lemon** (1966–). Gay. TV host.

- **Alvin Ailey, Jr.** (1931–1989). Gay. Founder, Alvin Ailey American Dance Theater in New York.

- **Josephine Baker** (1906–1975). Bisexual. Singer, dancer, actress, and activist. Significant contributions to the Civil Rights movement.

- **Rudolph Valentino** (1895–1926). Presumed gay. Famous actor in silent movies. Known as the Latin Lover. Married twice to women who presumably had lesbian relationships.

- **Marlon Brando** (1924–2004). Presumed bisexual. Actor. Named by the American Film Institute as the fourth greatest male American actor of all times. The book *Brando Unzipped* claims he had relationships with other famous actors, including James Dean, Cary Grant, John Gielgud, and Montgomery Clift.

- **Cary Grant** (1904–1986). Bisexual. Actor. The American Film Institute named him the Greatest Male Star of All Time. Movies: *The Philadelphia Story; To Catch a Thief; An Affair to Remember; North by Northwest...*

- **Sir John Gielgud** (1904–2000). Gay. Actor, director, producer. One of few to win an Oscar, a Tony, an Emmy, and a Grammy.

- **Montgomery Clift** (1920–1966). Bisexual. Actor: *From Here to Eternity, A Place in the Sun, Confess,* and more. Nominated four times for Academy Awards.

- **Greta Garbo** (1905–1990). Bisexual. Actress: *Anna Christie, Grand Hotel.*

- **James Dean** (1931–1955). Gay. Iconic actor: *Rebel Without a Cause, East of Eden,* and *Giant.*

- **Anthony Perkins** (1932–1992). Gay. Oscar-winning actor. Died of AIDS.

- **Jodie Foster** (1962–). Lesbian. Actress, film director, and producer.

- **Sir Laurence Olivier** (1907–1989). Presumed bisexual. Renowned actor and director.

- **Tab Hunter** (1931–). Gay. Actor: *Battle Cry, That Kind of Woman.*

- **Suze Orman** (1951–). Lesbian. Financial advisor, author, TV host.

- **David Geffen** (1943–). Gay. Film, theater, and music producer: *ET* and *Saving Private Ryan,* and more.

- **Chaz Bono** (1969–). Transgender. Writer and musician. Child of entertainers Sonny and Cher.

- **Ismail Merchant** (1936–2005) and **James Ivory** (1928–). Gay couple. Founders, Merchant Ivory productions. Films: *A Room with a View, Maurice, Mr. and Mrs. Bridge, Howards End.*

- **Pier Paolo Pasolini** (1922–1975). Gay. Film director and writer. Films: *Teorema, Canterbury Tales.*

- **Luchino Visconti** (1906–1976). Gay. Film, opera, and theater director. Films include *Death in Venice, The Leopard,* and *The Dammed.*

- **Pedro Almodóvar** (1949–). Gay. Oscar-winning Spanish filmmaker: *All About My Mother. Talk to Her.*

- **Lana Wachowski** (1965–). Transgender. Working as a team with brother Andy, they are filmmakers, screenwriters, and producers: The *Matrix* series of movies, and others.

CIVIC ENGAGEMENT

- **Harry Hay** (1912–2002). Gay. Renowned LGBT rights activist. Cofounder: Mattachine Society, Radical Faeries.

- **Del Martin** (1921–2008) and **Phyllis Lyon** (1924–). Lesbian couple. Renowned feminists and gay-rights activists. Founders of Daughters of Bilitis.

- **Frank Kameny** (1925–2011). Gay. Astronomer. Activist. Created slogan *"Gay is Good."*

- **Bayard Rustin** (1912–1987). Gay. Civil rights leader. Main organizer of the 1983 March on Washington.

- **Jane Addams** (1860–1935). Lesbian. First American woman to win the Nobel Peace Prize (1931).

- **Leonard Matlovich** (1943–1988). Gay. Vietnam War veteran, Purple Heart and Bronze Star. Tombstone reads: "A Gay Vietnam Veteran—When I was in the military, they gave me a medal for killing two men and a discharge for loving one."

- **Roberta Achtenberg** (1950–). Lesbian. First openly LGBT person whose appointment required US Senate confirmation (1993, asst. secretary of Housing and Urban Development). Currently, commissioner, US Commission on Civil Rights.

- **Chai Feldblum** (1959–). Lesbian. Professor of law, Georgetown University. Chair, Equal Employment Opportunity Commission.

- **Axel and Eigil Axgil** (Axel: 1915–2011; Eigil: 1922–1995). Gay. First gay couple in the world to be joined in a registered domestic partnership (Denmark, 1989).

- **Ann Bancroft** (1955–). Lesbian. Adventurer, teacher, author. First woman to reach the North Pole by foot and sled. First woman to cross both the North and South Poles. First woman to ski across Greenland.

- **Deborah Batts** (1947–). Lesbian. First openly LGBT, African-American federal judge.

- **Baron Baden Powell** (1857–1941). Presumed gay. Army officer and writer. Considered the founder of the International Scouting Movement (Boy Scouts).

- **Laurence Michael Dillon** (1915–1962). Transgender. Physician, aristocrat, and first female-to-male transgender individual to undergo phalloplasty. Author: *Self—A Study in Endocrinology and Ethics.*

In addition, there are many other people who are committed to achieving equality for lesbian, gay, bisexual and transgender people. Here are just a few of them:

FOUNDERS OF NEW ORGANIZATIONS FOR EQUALITY (last 10 years)

- **Juan and Ken Ahonen-Jover** (eQualityGiving)

- **Tico Almeida** (Freedom to Work)

- **Wayne Besen** (Truth Wins Out)

- **Dana Beyer and Sharon Brackett** (Gender Rights Maryland)

- **David Brock** (EqualityMatters)

- **Linda Bush** (Movement Advancement Project)

- **Mitchell Gold and Jimmy Creech** (Faith in America)

- **Georg Ketelhohn and Heddy Pena + 12 more** (Florida Together)

- **Carolyn Laub** (Gay Straight Alliance Network)

- **Robyn McGeehe and Kip Williams** (GetEqual)

- **Dan Savage** (It Gets Better)

- **Josh Seefried and Ty Walrod** (OutServe, which is merging with SLDN)

- **Chuck Williams** (The Williams Institute)

- **Shane Windmeyer, Chad Wilson,** and **Sarah Holmes** (Campus Pride)

HEADS OF MAJOR NATIONAL ORGANIZATIONS FOR EQUALITY

- **Michael Adams** (Services and Advocacy for LGBT Elders, SAGE)

- **Aaron Belkin** (Palm Center)

- **Eliza Byard** (Gay Lesbian & Straight Education Network, GLSEN)

- **Rea Carey** (The Task Force)

- **Kevin Cathcart** (Lambda Legal)

- **Jennifer Chrisler** (Family Equality Council)

- **Clarke Cooper** (Log Cabin Republicans, LCR)

- **Jerame Davis** (National Stonewall Democrats, NSD)

- **Masen Davis** (Transgender Law Center)

- **James Esseks** (American Civil Liberties Union LGBT Project)

- **Herndon Graddick** (GLAAD)

- **Chad Griffin** (Human Rights Campaign, HRC)

- **Jody Huckaby** (Parents, Families and Friends of Lesbians and Gays, PFLAG)

- **Rebecca Isaacs** (Equality Federation)

- **Mara Keisling** (National Center for Transgender Equality, NCTE)

- **Kate Kendell** (National Center for Lesbian Rights, NCLR)

- **Sharon Lettman-Hicks** (National Black Justice Coalition, NBJC)

- **Abbe Land** (The Trevor Project)

- **Ricci Levy** (Woodhull Sexual Freedom Alliance)

- **Allyson Robinson** (OutServe-SLDN)

- **Peggy Shorey** (Pride at Work)

- **Terry Stone** (CenterLink)

- **Lee Swislow** (Gay & Lesbian Advocates & Defenders, GLAD)

- **Rachel Tiven** (Immigration Equality)

- **Adam Umboefer** (American Foundation for Equal Rights, AFER)

- **Chuck Wolfe** (Victory Fund)

- **Evan Wolfson** (Freedom to Marry)

ACTIVISTS AND DONORS WHO ARE MAKING A DIFFERENCE

- **Henry van Ameringen,** strategic donor
- **Ron Ansin,** strategic donor
- **Chip Arndt,** activist and *Amazing Race* winner
- **John Bare,** activist donor
- **Jarrett Barrios,** strategist
- **Vic Basile,** strategist
- **Ignatius Bau,** strategist
- **Dana Beyer,** transgender activist and political candidate
- **Adam Bink,** grassroots activist
- **Brian Bond,** White House liaison

- **Mary Bonauto,** legal super ace
- **Marsha Botzer,** transgender activist
- **Jeff Campagna,** activist
- **Tom Carpenter,** strategist
- **Mandy Carter,** activist and Nobel Prize nominee
- **Jerry Chasen,** activist donor
- **Dan Choi,** DADT and equality activist
- **Bobby Clark,** online activist
- **Kate Clinton,** comedian
- **Michael Coe,** communicator
- **Matt Coles,** legal strategist
- **David da Silva Cornell,** activist
- **Anna Curren,** repeal DADT donor
- **Erin Drinkwater,** activist and doer
- **Stephen Driscoll,** democratic activist
- **Liebe and Seth Gadinsky,** allied donors
- **Brian Gaither,** activist
- **Chris Gates,** activist
- **Ethan Geto,** communications strategist
- **Don George,** activist donor
- **Lila Gracey,** strategist
- **Joe Falk,** political donor
- **J. Todd "Tif" Fernandez,** grassroots activist
- **Matt Foreman,** strategist
- **Nathaniel Frank,** author
- **Stephen Handwerk,** Democratic activist
- **Craig Harwood,** donor and producer
- **Yashar Hedayat,** strategic donor
- **Stephen Herbits,** strategic doer, and donor
- **Joanne Herman,** transgender educator
- **Daniel Hernandez,** helping hand
- **Kelly Rivera Hart,** Latino and bi activist
- **Steve Hildebrand,** strategist
- **Donald Hitchcock,** strategist and activist
- **Ernest Hopkins,** activist
- **Bob Horvath,** political activist
- **Lane Hudson,** communications strategist and provocateur
- **Kathy James,** family advocate
- **Brian Johnson,** activist
- **Corey Johnson,** activist and political candidate
- **Hans Johnson,** activist
- **Michael Kenny,** strategist and connector
- **Norm Kent,** publisher
- **Jon Kislak,** allied donor

- **Geoff Kors,** strategist
- **Lisa Kove,** Department of Defense activist
- **Michael Krawitz,** strategic donor
- **Janice Langbehn,** activist and 2011 US presidential Citizens medal recipient
- **Andrew Lane,** foundation executive director
- **Jeff Lewy,** activist donor
- **Kerry Lobel,** strategist
- **Bill Lyons,** donor advisor
- **Barbara McCullough-Jones,** activist
- **Stuart Milk,** international activist
- **Richard Milstein,** donor
- **Shannon Price Minter,** transgender legal ace
- **Ineke Mushovic,** strategist
- **Kathryn Natale and Janet McLeod,** strategic donors
- **Christopher Neff,** journalist and publisher
- **Richard Noble,** walking activist
- **Derek Newton,** allied campaign strategist
- **CJ Ortuno,** activist ally
- **Dixon Osburn,** strategist
- **Kathy Padilla,** transgender activist
- **Jim Pepper,** strategic donor
- **Catherine Pino** and **Ingrid Duran,** strategists
- **Libby Post,** communicator
- **Bruce Presley,** donor and producer
- **Lisa Polyak,** marriage activist
- **Donna Red Wing,** activist leader
- **Cathy Renna,** communications expert
- **Alix Ritchie and Marty Davis,** agitators
- **Laura Ricketts,** strategic donor
- **Cindy Rizzo,** human sexuality activist
- **Charles Robbins,** youth advocate
- **Mike Rogers,** blogger and citizen reporter
- **Charlie Rounds** and **Mark Hiemenz,** maverick donors
- **Hilary Rosen,** strategist
- **Marty Rouse,** grassroots activist
- **Caitlin Ryan,** family advocate and researcher
- **Rebecca Salokar,** professor and strategist
- **Diego Sanchez,** transgender activist
- **Marsha Scott,** donor strategist
- **Eugene Sepulveda,** donor
- **Garry Shay,** Democratic activist
- **Joel Silberman,** media strategist
- **Howard Simon,** allied defender

- **Maryann Simpson,** donor
- **Barbra "Babs" Casbar Siperstein,** political compromiser
- **Richard Socarides,** activist
- **Palm Spaulding,** blogger
- **Rick Stafford,** Democratic activist
- **Anne Stanback,** marriage activist
- **Mark Steinberg** and **Dennis Edwards,** donors
- **Jim Stork,** strategist and donor
- **Sean Strub,** HIV activist
- **Andrew Sullivan,** author
- **Andy Szekeres,** fundraiser
- **Maxim Thorne,** strategist
- **Lisa Turner,** strategist
- **Urvashi Vaid,** author and strategist
- **Leoni Walker,** donor
- **Jillian Weiss,** transgender activist
- **Bernard Whitman,** communications expert
- **Sara Whitman,** activist donor
- **Jon Winkleman,** political activist
- **Bob Witeck,** communications expert
- **Paul Yandura,** donor strategist and revolutionary
- **Rich Yurko,** activist

APPENDIX 2:

The Dallas Principles

Below is the full text of the Dallas Principles (available at TheDallasPrinciples.com).

It is composed of: preamble, principles, full civil rights goals, and a call to action. The list of authors follows.

PREAMBLE

President Obama and Congress pledged to lead America in a new direction that included civil rights for lesbian, gay, bisexual and transgender Americans. We now sit at a great moment in our history that inspires the nation to return to its highest ideals and greatest promise. We face a historic opportunity to obtain our full civil rights; this is the moment for change. No delay. No excuses.

Nearly forty years ago, a diverse group of lesbian, gay, bisexual, and transgender people stood up to injustice at the Stonewall Inn in New York City. In doing so, they submitted themselves to bodily harm and criminal prosecution. Their demand was simple—equal protection under the law.

Still today, full civil rights has eluded the same community that rioted forty years ago. Instead, untold sums of resources have been spent to divide our nation and turn our lives into a political football.

At several junctures in American history, the stars have aligned to deliver the promise of equal protection under the law to those previously denied. At this unique time in history, our nation must once again exercise the great tradition of making its people equal.

Justice has too long been delayed. A clear path toward full civil equality for the LGBT community is overdue and must come now.

Using fear and misunderstanding to justify discrimination is no longer acceptable in this nation. Those content with the way things are will be judged harshly by history. Those who do not actively advance these ideals or offer excuses will be judged just as harshly. Those who attempt to divide our community or to delay and deny action on civil equality, waiting for the right moment to arrive, will be held accountable.

We reject the idea that honoring the founding principles of our country is controversial. We believe in the inherent human dignity of all people. No longer will we submit our children, our family, our friends, and ourselves as a political tool for any Party or ideology. A new day has arrived.

PRINCIPLES

The following eight guiding principles underlie our call to action. In order to achieve full civil rights now, we avow:

1. Full civil rights for lesbian, gay, bisexual and transgender individuals must be enacted now. Delay and excuses are no longer acceptable.

2. We will not leave any part of our community behind.

3. Separate is never equal.

4. Religious beliefs are not a basis upon which to affirm or deny civil rights.

5. The establishment and guardianship of full civil rights is a non-partisan issue.

6. Individual involvement and grassroots action are paramount to success and must be encouraged.

7. Success is measured by the civil rights we all achieve, not by words, access or money raised.

8. Those who seek our support are expected to commit to these principles.

FULL CIVIL RIGHTS GOALS

Being united by common principles and engaging in united action, we will achieve the following goals:

1. DIGNITY AND EQUALITY. Every lesbian, gay, bisexual, and transgender person has inherent dignity and worth, and has the right to live free of discrimination and harassment.

2. FAMILY. Every LGBT person has the right to a family without legal barriers to immigration, civil marriage, or raising children.

3. ECONOMIC OPPORTUNITY. Every LGBT person has the right to economic opportunity free from discrimination in employment, public housing, accommodation, public facilities, credit, and federally funded programs and activities.

4. EDUCATION. Every LGBT child and youth has the right to an education that is affirming, inclusive, and free from bullying.

5. NATIONAL SECURITY. Every LGBT person should have the opportunity to serve our

country openly and equally in our military and foreign service.

6. CRIME. Every LGBT person should enjoy life protected against bias crimes.

7. HEALTHCARE. Every person should have access to affordable, high quality, and culturally competent healthcare without discrimination.

CALL TO ACTION

1. We demand that government officials act now to achieve full civil rights without delay.

2. Our organizations and individuals need to develop a collaborative and revolutionary new organizing model that mobilizes millions of supporters through emerging web and phone technologies.

3. All LGBT individuals must accept personal responsibility to do everything within their power for equality and should get involved in the movement by volunteering, giving and being out.

4. We will hold elected officials and our organizations accountable for being transparent and achieving full civil rights by active participation when possible and active opposition when necessary.

5. Our allies need to be proactive in public support for full civil rights.

6. Every government measure that quantifies the US citizenry must permit LGBT individuals to self-identify and be counted in every way citizens are counted.

7. We demand that the media present LGBT lives in fair, accurate, and objective ways that neither include nor give credence to unsubstantiated, discriminatory claims and opinions.

AUTHORS

Here are the authors of the Dallas Principles with their affiliations at the time that the principles were written.

- **Dr. Juan Ahonen-Jover,** cofounder of eQualityGiving

- **Dr. Ken Ahonen-Jover,** cofounder of eQualityGiving

- **John Bare,** activist donor

- **Senator Jarrett Barrios,** former Massachusetts legislator

- **Dr. Dana Beyer,** transgender and political activist

- **Jeff Campagna, Esq.,** attorney and LGBT fundraiser and organizer

- **Mandy Carter,** Nobel Peace Prize nominee and lesbian activist

- **Michael Coe,** one of the "Most Influential Washingtonians under the Age of 40" according to *Washington Life Magazine*

- **Rev. Jimmy Creech,** straight ally working to end religion-based bigotry

- **Allison Duncan,** donor advisor

- **Ambassador Michael Guest,** senior advisor to the Council for Global Equality

- **Joanne Herman,** donor and transgender rights advocate

- **Donald Hitchcock,** activist and former executive director, Gay and Lesbian Leadership Council

- **Lane Hudson,** political activist and one of the "Most Influential Gay People in America" according to *Out Magazine*

- **Charles Merrill,** philanthropist (Merrill-Lynch family), activist, and artist

- **Dixon Osburn, Esq.,** cofounder, former executive director, Servicemembers Legal Defense Network

- **Lisa Polyak,** lead plaintiff in litigation to obtain marriage equality in Maryland

- **Babs Casbar Siperstein,** transgender activist and board member

- **Pam Spaulding,** editor and publisher, PamsHouseBlend.com

- **Andy Szekeres,** political consultant and fundraiser

- **Lisa Turner,** political consultant and donor advisor

- **Jon Winkleman,** political activist

- **Paul Yandura,** political strategist and donor advisor

APPENDIX 3:

Good Companies

Listed below by industry are the companies with a 100-percent rating in the 2013 Corporate Equality Index compiled by the Human Rights Campaign (www.hrc.org/cei). Note that this list is not exhaustive since there might be companies with a 100-percent rating that have not reported to the Human Rights Campaign.

ADVERTISING AND MARKETING
- Digitas (new)
- Interpublic Group of Companies (new)
- Publicis (new)
- Razorfish (new)
- Starcom MediaVest Group (new)

AEROSPACE AND DEFENSE
- Lockheed Martin
- Raytheon

AIRLINES
- AMR Corp. (American Airlines)
- United Continental Holdings

APPAREL, FASHION, TEXTILES, DEPARTMENT STORES
- Levi Strauss & Co.
- Nike

AUTOMOTIVE
- Chrysler
- Ford
- General Motors (new)
- Toyota
- Wolkswagen Group of America (new)

BANKING AND FINANCIAL SERVICES
- American Express

- Ameriprise Financial
- Bank of America
- Bank of New York Mellon
- Barclays
- BlacRock (new)
- BMO Bankcorp
- BNP Paribas (new)
- Capital One
- Charles Schwab
- Citigroup
- Credit Suisse USA
- Depository Trust & Clearing Corp. (new)
- Deutsche Bank
- Freddie Mac
- Goldman Sachs
- HSBC - North America (new)
- JP Morgan Chase
- KeyCorp (new)
- MasterCard (new)
- Moody's (new)
- Morgan Stanley
- Northern Trust
- PNC Financial Services Group (new)
- RBC Wealth Management (new)
- SunTrust Banks (new)
- TD Bank
- Teachers Insurance & Annuity Association
- Toyota Financial Services
- US Bancorp
- UBS AG
- Wells Fargo

CHEMICALS AND BIOTECHNOLOGY
- Dow Chemical
- Ecolab (new)
- Genentech
- Monsanto (new)

COMPUTER AND DATA SERVICES
- Automatic Data Processing
- Broadridge Financial Solutions (new)
- EMC
- Hewlett-Packard

COMPUTER HARDWARE AND OFFICE EQUIPMENT
- Apple
- Dell
- Lexmark International (new)
- Tech Data Corp.
- Xerox

COMPUTER SOFTWARE
- CA Inc. (new)
- Electronic Arts (new)
- Intuit
- Microsoft
- Oracle
- Symantec

CONSULTING AND BUSINESS SERVICES
- A.T. Kearney
- Accenture
- Aon
- Bain & Co.
- Booz Allen Hamilton
- Boston Consulting Group
- Deloitte
- Ernst & Young
- IBM
- KPMG
- Marsh & McLennan Companies
- McKinsey & Co.
- Navigant Consulting
- PricewaterhouseCoopers

EDUCATION AND CHILD CARE
No companies in this industry reporting 100 percent rating

ENERGY AND UTILITIES
- Exelon
- PG&E
- Sempra Energy
- Southern California Edison

ENGINEERING AND CONSTRUCTION
No companies in this industry reporting 100 percent rating

ENTERTAINMENT AND ELECTRONIC MEDIA
- AMC Entertainment (new)
- Comcast (new)
- Sony Pictures Entertainment (new)
- Time Warner
- Walt Disney

FOOD, BEVERAGES AND GROCERIES
- Brown-Forman
- Cargill
- Coca-Cola
- Darden Restaurants (new)
- Delhaize America
- Diageo North America
- E&J Gallo Winery (new)
- General Mills
- Kellogg
- Kraft Foods
- MillerCoors
- PepsiCo (new)
- Sodexo
- Supervalu

FOREST AND PAPER PRODUCTS
No companies in this industry reporting 100 percent rating

HEALTHCARE / HEALTH INSURANCE
- Aetna
- Blue Cross Blue Shield of Minnesota
- Cardinal Health
- CIGNA (new)
- Group Health Cooperative
- Kaiser Permanente (new)
- UnitedHealth Group

HEALTHCARE / MEDICAL FACILITIES
No companies in this industry reporting 100 percent rating

HIGH-TECH / PHOTO / SCIENCE EQUIPMENT
- Cisco
- Eastman Kodak
- Medtronic
- Nokia

HOME FURNISHING
- Mitchell Gold + Bob Williams

HOTELS, RESORTS AND CASINOS
- Caesars Entertainment
- Choice Hotels International
- Hyatt Hotels
- Kimpton Hotel & Restaurant Group
- MGM Resorts (new)
- Starwood Hotels & Resorts
- Wyndham Worldwide (new)
- Wynn Resorts (new)

INSURANCE
- AAA Northern California, Nevada & Utah Insurance
- AIG (new)
- Blue Cross and Blue Shield of Florida
- Chubb
- Hartford Financial Services (new)
- Harvard Pilgrim Health Care (new)
- ING North America Insurance
- MedLife
- Nationwide
- Progressive (new)
- Prudential Financial
- Sun Life Financial (U.S.)

INTERNET SERVICES AND RETAILING
- eBay
- Google
- Yahoo!

LAW FIRMS
Seventy-one law firms report a 100 percent rating (sixteen more than in 2012)

MAIL AND FREIGHT DELIVERY
No companies in this industry reporting 100 percent rating

MANUFACTURING
- Corning
- Cummins
- Herman Miller
- Owens Corning

- Rockwell Automation (new)
- United Technologies
- Whirlpool

MINING AND METALS
- Alcoa

MISCELLANEOUS
- Thomson Reuters (new)

OIL AND GAS
- Chevron

PHARMACEUTICALS
- Boehringer Ingelheim USA (new)
- Bristol-Myers Squibb
- Eli Lilly
- GlaxoSmithKline
- Johnson & Johnson
- Merck (new)
- Novartis Pharmaceuticals (new)
- Pfizer

PUBLISHING AND PRINTING
No companies in this industry reporting 100 percent rating

REAL ESTATE, RESIDENTIAL
No companies in this industry reporting 100 percent rating

RETAIL AND CONSUMER PRODUCTS
- 3M
- Abercrombie & Fitch
- Avon
- Barnes & Noble
- Best Buy
- Clorox
- GameStop (new)
- Gap
- Limited Brands
- Nordstrom
- Office Depot
- Replacements
- S.C. Johnson & Son (new)
- Sears

- Staples
- TJX
- Uniliver
- Walgreens (new)

TELECOMMUNICATIONS
- Alcatel-Lucent
- AT&T
- Sprint
- Verizon (new)

TOBACCO
No companies in this industry reporting 100 percent rating

TRANSPORTATION AND TRAVEL
- Orbitz

WASTE MANAGEMENT
No companies in this industry reporting 100 percent rating